Dark Peak Aircraft Wrecks 1 REVISED

Ron Collier
Roni Wilkinson

LEO COOPER
LONDON

First published in 1979 by
The Barnsley Chronicle Newspaper Group

Republished in this edition 1990, by
Wharncliffe Publishing Limited

Reprinted 1995, by
LEO COOPER Ltd
190 Shaftesbury Avenue, London WC2H 8JL
an imprint of Pen & Sword Books Ltd
47 Church Street, Barnsley, S. Yorkshire S70 2AS

Front cover painting by Paul Morton depicts
Sabres of 66 Squadron XD730 and XD707 flown
by Alan Green and Jim Horne (story
on page 81).

*For up-to date information on other titles produced under
the Leo Cooper imprint, please telephone or write to:*

      Pen & Sword Books Ltd
      FREEPOST
      47 Church Street
      Barnsley
      South Yorkshire S70 2BR
      Telephone (24 hours): 01226 734555

ISBN: 0 85052 457 1

A CIP catalogue record of this book is available
from the British Library

Printed in Great Britain by
Redwood Books Limited
Trowbridge, Wiltshire

This book is dedicated to the memory of my dear friend and constant walking companion, Ken Kershaw, whose original idea this book was. Ken was killed by lightning, Sunday May 1st 1988, whilst hill walking on Caer Caradoc, Shropshire.

Contents

INTRODUCTION

In the second half of the seventies we undertook to publish a series of articles in The Barnsley Chronicle Newspaper Group of weekly newspapers. Little did we realise at the time the amount of interest the series would arouse.

The stories were based upon information submitted by Glossop historian, Mr Ron Collier. Years of research by him had uncovered information behind the aircraft wreck sites scattered throughout the Peak District National Park. Our art department compiled the stories, illustrated the series, and over the months the accounts appeared in all our titles during the seventies. Requests for back issues of the papers carrying the stories, came in from parts of the country well out of our circulation area and stocks were soon exhausted. To cope with the demand for stories we quickly produced a booklet, which sold out in a matter of months. Rather than do a reprint it was decided to wait until the stories had been further researched — Ron Collier set out to locate more survivors and next of kin. It has taken him twelve years to make a detailed search and the update is presented here.

In 1982 a more substantial book was published by us covering the stories that had been thoroughly researched and for which, it was considered, little extra material would come to light. The releasing of that second book, *Dark Peak Aircraft Wrecks Book 2 by Ron Collier*, only served to arouse further interest in the stories contained in the first booklet. We were surprised to learn that copies of that first booklet were much sought after and were changing hands at an inflated price.

We are now pleased to publish Book 1 with filled out and updated material, along with seven additional stories and thus complete the epic.

Both publications are a fitting memorial to those who lost their lives in flying accidents in the Peak District National Park. Their memory is perpetuated in the photographs of individuals along with their stories. We feel sure that relatives of those who lost their lives will be grateful to the author for his years of dedication in unearthing the true accounts behind the Dark Peak Aircraft Wrecks.

Sir Nicholas Hewitt, Bt.
CHAIRMAN AND MANAGING DIRECTOR

ACKNOWLEDGEMENTS

I would like to express my appreciation and thanks for all the help and co-operation given to me by survivors and next of kin, without whose assistance many stories would have gone untold. Filling in the backgrounds to the events recorded in this work has been possible because of the help rendered by ex-squadron members. Also ready to assist me were ex-members of the local mountain rescue unit, based at Harpur Hill, Buxton. The team at Buxton attended 88 crashes over a period of three war years. The founder member of the team, Air Commodore David Crichton, MBE, and his daughter Penny Buckley, have proved a valuable source of information in compiling these acounts.

My thanks to Peggy Davis and the trustees of the *Glossop Heritage Centre* for the assistance in establishing a permanent memorial scroll, along with an exhibition, in Glossop. This is to perpetuate the memory of all allied airmen who lost their lives in the hills of Derbyshire.

Also my thanks go to all the members of the *Glossop Aviation Archaeological Society*, who over the many years of foot slogging have contributed so much to this subject.

The following departments and their staffs have rendered invaluable help over the years: *Air Historical Branch, MOD*, London; *RAF Officers' Branch*, Barnwood; *RAF Airmens' Branch*, Innsworth; *RAF Museum*, Hendon; *RAF Association*, London; *Naval Historical Branch*, London; *Imperial War Museum*, London; *Public Records Office*, Kew; *Commonwealth War Graves Commission*, Maidenhead; *Newark Air Museum; Board of Trade Accident Investigations*, London; *Public Archives of Canada*, Ottawa; *Commonwealth Air Training Plan Museum*, Manitoba; *Australian Department of Defence, AF Personnel*, Canberra; *New Zealand Air Force Relations Officer*, Nelson; *Polish Air Force Association*, London; *Belgian Air Force Association*, Brussels; *US Air Force Inspection and Safety Center*, Norton AFB, California, USA; *Albert F. Simpson Historical Center*, Maxwell AFB, Alabama, USA; *US General Services Administration*, Washington DC; *Smithsonian Institution, Information Management Division*, Washington DC; *The Boeing Company, Historical Services*, Seattle; *United States Air Force Museum*, Wright-Patterson AF Base, Ohio; *BAD Two Newsletter*, Delaware, USA.

The following individuals gave of their time and expertise:

Paul and Tom Allonby; Charles Austin; John Austin; Ken Bancroft; Stan Bishop; Barry Blunt; John Broomhead; H. P. Budgen; Paul Connatty; Eddie Doylrush; George Finn; Roger Freeman; Pete Foard, ex 66 Squadron; *Brian Gillard; John Hamer; Joe Harrington,* ex 66 Squadron; *Les Hayward,* ex 66 Squadron; *Fred Hoddinott; Philippa Hodgkis; Harry Holmes; Bernard Howard,* ex 66 Squadron; *Roy and Joyce Inkester,* Toronto; *Russel Ives; Mike Jakeman,* Ontario; *Alan Jones; Dick Kinder,* USA; *Mike Lawton; Air Commodore R. R. Lewis; Roger Lindsay; Larry Milberry,* Publisher, Ontario; *David Morse,* USA; *Leroy Nitschkke,* USA; *Sheena Oakley; C. W. Pridgeon; Madam Risseghem,* Belgium; *R. L. Robertson; Brian Robinson,* Manchester Airport Archivist; *Bill Russell,* USA; *Gerald Scarrett; Ron Seymour; Bob Shnug* USA; *David Smith; Gerald Sokl; Bernard Stevens; Air Commodore D. M. Strong; Charlie Sutcliffe; F. Tasker; Kenneth Tinker; Ken Thompson; Air Commodore Wake; Dick Walker; Herbert Ward; Norman Winterbottom; Harry Woolhouse.*

In expressing gratitude to all who have helped me, it would be a serious omission not mention my wife Susan, who has supported me throughout, despite having little interest in the subject of aviation.

BIBLIOGRAPHY

The Canadair Sabre by Larry Milberry, Canav Books.
The Secret Squadrons by Robert Jackson, Robson Books Ltd.
Bomber Squadrons of the RAF by Philip Moyes, MacDonald and James (Publishers) Ltd.
Fly and Deliver by Hugh Bergel, Airlife Publishing Ltd.

Lancaster KB993, 408 Squadron RCAF, flying 'circuits and bumps' at Linton-on-Ouse crashed on James's Thorn, 18th May, 1945. **Map reference 077949 • Map key number 1**

The badge of 408 Squadron had upon it a Canadian goose in full flight and bore the badge motto 'For Freedom'. The Canadian squadron had been formed at Lindholme in 1941, the second of many RCAF bomber squadrons that were to serve overseas. Its first operation was against railway marshalling yards in June 1941, and when the first 1000 bomber raid was launched against the German city of Cologne in May 1942, 408 (Goose) Squadron took part, flying Hampdens.

The war in Europe had ended just ten days earlier, when Lancaster KB993 took off for its last flight, a quick flip that was to wipe out all but one member of a crew that had survived the fierce air war over Europe. Their last operational flight against Hitler's crumbling Third Reich had taken place over a week earlier when nine Lancasters bombed the Fuhrer's home at Berchtesgaden, and four other crews bombed enemy gun batteries on the island of Wangerooge.

With the end of hostilities Goose Squadron had been re-equipped with brand new Lancaster X's. The crews were to fly the Canadian built bombers back home and spirits were high as the day drew closer for the Squadron's departure. An 'open home' day had been organised for the 20th, when locals and others were invited to visit the station prior to the Canadians leaving.

Meanwhile Group HQ was hard put to find fresh activities for the crews. Cross country flights and fighter affiliation exercises had been carried out, then there was the inevitable 'circuits and bumps' training. Routine and dull stuff for crews who had survived the war and were four weeks away from setting off on the long journey home.

In the early evening of 18th May, Lancaster EQ-U with Flying Officer Anthony Arthur Clifford at the controls took off from Linton-on-Ouse. The crew consisted of Bomb Aimer, Flying Officer David (Scratch) Fehrman; Wireless Operator, Warrant Officer Michael Cecil (Blood and Guts) Cameron; Air Gunner, Flight Sergeant Clarence (Hairless Joe) Halvorson; Air Gunner, Flight Sergeant Leslie Claude (Rabbit) Hellerson and Flight Engineer, Pilot Officer Kenneth (Gassless) McIver. The navigator, 'Gee Sam', was not on board, but the crew were only cleared for local flying so his skills would not be required.

At around 10 pm Lancaster KB993 was circling over the town of Glossop, some 50 miles from the airfield at Linton. With daylight gone and no navigator on board, Clifford must have been attempting to establish his position when he flew into the mountain top.

It would seem that the crew, bored with flying round practising landings and take-offs, with no fixed exercise, had decided to go for a circular tour. Darkness must have caught them out of sight of base and lost over the Derbyshire hills. The lights of the town of Glossop would have been visible to crew members as they circled overhead, as blackout restrictions had been lifted.

Mr Ken Bancroft was standing on the steps of his father's workshop watching the bomber as it circled around. It straightened and headed towards the east and the peaks which, in that area, rise to 2000 feet. He was still watching as the bomber struck the top of James's Thorn and burst into a ball of flame. He immediately ran off to the police station and reported what he had seen, but at first no one would believe him. Eventually, someone was sent off on a motorcycle to see if there was any truth in the young boy's story.

All the crew of six had perished in the crash, although the rear gunner lived for a short while. 408 (Goose) Squadron left for Canada on the 20th June, 1945, leaving one of its aircraft 'impaled' on James's Thorn.

Above: **Anthony Arthur Clifford,** RCAF, pilot of Lancaster KB993.

Below: *Fragments of the 408 Squadron Lancaster on James' Thorn. The town of Glossop can be seen in the distance.*

C-47 Skytrain, 2108982 of 32nd Troop Carrier Squadron, 314th Troop Carrier Group, USAAF, crashed Shelf Moor, 24th July, 1945.   **Map reference 082949 ● Map key number 2**

It was going on for 5 o'clock in the afternoon when Sergeant Pridgeon, an RAF cypher clerk, and his girl friend came upon the wreckage of a crashed aircraft. The sergeant lived nearby and most of his free time he spent walking the Derbyshire hills. He knew of the Lancaster bomber that had crashed at some point on the mountain top they were on, just nine weeks earlier. It looked as though they had come across what was left of the RCAF bomber.

The couple crossed over the sloping ground from the direction of Higher Shelf Stones towards the mounds of shattered metal. The significance of the white star and bars painted on the fuselage escaped Sergeant Pridgeon as he handed his camera to his girl friend. He walked over and stood with his back to the wreckage and called to his companion to take a picture, and to

make it a good one, as he had only one frame left.

She took the picture, lowered the camera, and called out that she had spotted someone asleep amongst the tufted grass. During his war service Sergeant Pridgeon had seen enough corpses to know at a glance that the crumpled figure in RAF uniform was in fact dead. He realised that they had come upon a new crash scene.

Turning from her, he proceeded to scramble in amongst the shattered metal and came upon the crew — all were dead. The RAF man must have been flung clear when the plane hit the mountain top, or he had crawled out and died.

Below: Photograph taken by Sergeant Pridgeon at the time that he discovered the crash. When he took this picture he was unaware that he was the first on the scene at a new tragic accident.

Skytrain (British named the C-47 the Dakota) had been carrying amongst its cargo a jeep. Upon impact the Jeep had torn loose from its securing ropes and had been hurled forward into the American occupants before bouncing up the moor. The sight of the mangled American crew was something that the lady would never forget.

The C-47 had taken off two days earlier on a routine supply trip from Leicester East to Renfrew in Scotland. The pilot, First Lieutenant George L. Johnson, had been warned of bad weather along the more direct flight path up central England. With predicted visability down to three miles as far as Glossop and a stationary cold front northwards from there as far as Scotland, an alternative flight path had been recommended. The pilot had been advised to fly up the East Coast so as to miss the Pennine mountains where cloud shrouded the hill tops.

The pilot must have decided to take the more direct route and risk the high ground. The rest of the five man crew consisted of co-pilot, First Lieutenant Earl W. Burns; navigator, First Lieutenant Beverly W. Izlar; Crew Chief, Sergeant Theodore R. McCrocklin and the radio operator, Sergeant Francis M. Maloney. There were two passengers, Corporal Grover R. Alexander, USAAF and RAF Leading Aircraftsman J. D. Main.

Above: *George L. Johnson,* USAAF, pilot of C-47 Skytrain 2108982.

Below: *The mangled remains of the Jeep that was being transported on board the C-47. Official USAAF photograph taken at the time.*

Superfortress RB-29A (F-13A) 44-61999 'Over Exposed' 16th Photographic Reconnaissance Squadron, 91st Reconnaissance Wing, 311th Air Division, Strategic Air Command. Formerly attached to 509th Composite Group (atomic bomb unit)Pacific. Crashed 3rd November, 1948. Higher Shelf Stones.

Map reference 090950 • Map key number 3

It was only a twenty five minute trip for a B-29 from Scampton in Lincolnshire to Burtonwood USAF base near Warrington. Prior to take-off on the morning of 3rd November, at around 10.15, the pilot Captain Landon P. Tanner, filed his Visual Flight Record with Flight Control for a routine flight. He was briefed that he would encounter broken clouds at 2,000 to 4,000 feet with visibility four to six miles.

His crew for the trip consisted of co-pilot, Captain Harry Stroud; engineer, Technical Sergeant Ralph Fields; navigator, Sergeant Charles Wilbanks; radio operator, Staff Sergeant Gene A. Gartner; radar operator, David D. Moore; camera crew, Technical Segeant Saul R. Banks, Sergeant Donald R. Abrogast, Sergeant Robert I. Doyle and Private First Class William M. Burrows. Two other crew members were Corporal M. Franssen and Corporal George Ingram. Acting as photographic advisor was Captain Howard Keel of the 4201st Motion Picture Unit.

Taken aboard the photo reconnaissance aircraft at Scampton was the

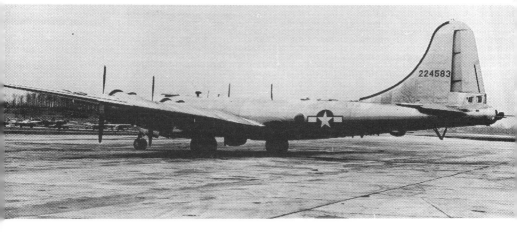

1st LT. Bob Murray   Capt. Ernie Mauck   Lou Hagemeyer

U.S. ARMY
ARMY AIR FORCES

1999

.000

Below: *This picture of 'Over Exposed' was taken at the time that the aircraft was involved in 'Operation Crossroads', the atomic bomb tests on Bikini Atoll in the summer of 1946.*

Above: *This photograph was taken at the time of the crash.*

payroll for the American staff at Burton-wood. Also sacks of mail homeward bound for the States was loaded in.

Around twenty minutes into the flight, Captain Tanner must have nosed down through the overcast to establish his position.

Shelf Moor rises to just over 2,000 feet above sea level — it is doubtful if any of the crew saw the ground before they hit it.

When Over Exposed failed to arrive at Burtonwood an air search was initiated and during that early wintery afternoon blazing wreckage was spotted.

By chance members of the Harpur Hill RAF Mountain Rescue Unit were just finishing an exercise two and a half miles away. They picked up the messages being broadcast by the search aircraft on their radio, to the effect that a 'Superfort' was down on the moor and burning. Checking the map reference Flight Sergeant George Thompson and Corporal William Duthie noted how close they were and promptly despatched the rest of the men to approach and search from one direction whilst they themselves started across the moor from Doctors Gate.

Mist and drizzle prevented them from spotting the aircraft at first, but after twenty minutes rough going over the raising moorland they could see the Superfort's huge tailfin and a fire blazing away in front of it.

The two of them raced the last few hundred yards stumbling into holes and jumping water courses. However, as they got close they could see that it was

Below: *Members of the the RAF Mountain Rescue Team based at Harpur Hill, seen here after their search for the Superfortress. Charles Austin, the team radio man, is pictured centre, along with Sergeant Thompson (far left) and Corporal W. Duthie (far right).*

Above: *The tail unit, much of it still intact; it was pulled over and chopped up shortly after this was taken.*

hopeless. Several bodies lay scattered around the blazing twisted metal, it was obvious that there was nothing that they could do for them and so they hurried back to their vehicle on the Snake Road.

Night was closing in as the Glossop firemen arrived at the crash site where wreckage spread across the moor for a quarter of a mile. Reinforcements from Harpur Hill arrived and a search was made for any survivors, but none were found - just eight bodies were located. They were left there as darkness fell and the rescuers made their way back to Glossop.

Next morning, before dawn, a group of around fifty men set off to the downed aircraft. Using torches and arc lamps they toiled back across the ravines and streams for two hours before the tailfin loomed up out of the grey dawn gloom. They now knew that thirteen men had been aboard, but they had only been able to gather eight bodies. Lines were formed to scour the moor for the missing five crew members.

Ted Ward was a member of the RAF Mountain Rescue Team from Harpur Hill, he recalled "The first piece of wreckage that I came across was the

Above: *One of the Wright Cyclone engines; in the days following the accident the site received the attention of many visitors. Before long the propellor blades had been cut away and removed by souvenir hunters.*

nose wheel, followed after some 200 hundred yards by the tail unit."

Another body was stumbled upon thrown clear of the wreckage, then American officers discovered the other four — Ted Ward was close by. "I was within two or three yards when the remaining four were found, unfortunately they were burned beyond recognition."

Scrambling about amongst the wreckage one of the American officers located a 'Wells-Fargo' style satchel which contained £7,000, part of the payroll, "This is what we're looking for," he called to the others.

How to get the bodies off the moor was the next problem that they had to face. Because of the rough terrain it was suggested that rather than carry the stretchers three miles across the moors to the Snake Pass Road, they would call in helicopters. However, the rescue men volunteered to attempt the job themselves. Six men to a stretcher they set off down the moorland with others taking turns to carry the grim loads.

The bodies were taken on to Burtonwood Air Force Base, which at that period served as a servicing depot for American aircraft engaged in the Berlin airlift.

Above: *This time piece taken from the wrist of one of the crew members was used to establish the time of the crash.*

Below: *Langdon P. Tanner, USAF, pilot of 'Over Exposed'. The photograph was taken early during his flying training.*

17

The crew of Over Exposed had completed their service in Britain and were due to return home to the States in three days time.

Captain Langdon P. Tanner, pilot of Over Exposed was 33 when he died, leaving a wife Erma and two small girls, Jean and Jane. He had joined the forces in 1936 and spent the war in the States. When ther war ended he was engaged in ferrying B-29s for storage.

When the Russians closed the road link into the Allied Sector of Berlin in 1948, supplies were flown in by air. Some 90 Superfortresses were then based in Britain. Over Exposed was a F-13A photo reconnaissance aircraft which could mingle with the vast flow of air traffic flying over Russian-held territory. Whilst the transports flew in fuel and food to the Allied Sector of Berlin, 16th Photographic Reconnaissance Squadron 'mapped' the Russian occupied territory.

The photo reconnaissance role of the B-29 began in March 1944, when the Development Engineering Branch of the

Air Staff in Washington DC directed that an engineering study be initiated to determine the practicability of installing cameras.

Using six cameras in the rear pressurised compartment a strip of ground three miles wide could be photographed. A photo navigator's station in the nose of the aircraft occupied the bombardier's position and was in direct communication with the camera station in the waist.

The bomb bays were utilised to the best possible extent by fitting extra fuel tanks. Thus modified it was no longer a B-29 but was now designated a F-13.

On June 15th, 1944 the first B-29 attack on Japan took place. The crews were briefed for the raid from photographs, in some cases, fifteen years old. With the heavy bomber onslaught on the Japanese mainland well underway the Bombardment Groups needed up to date intelligence — the need for the F-13 became urgent. Finally after many delays the F-13 entered service in November 1944 when the first two F-13s arrived in Saipan.

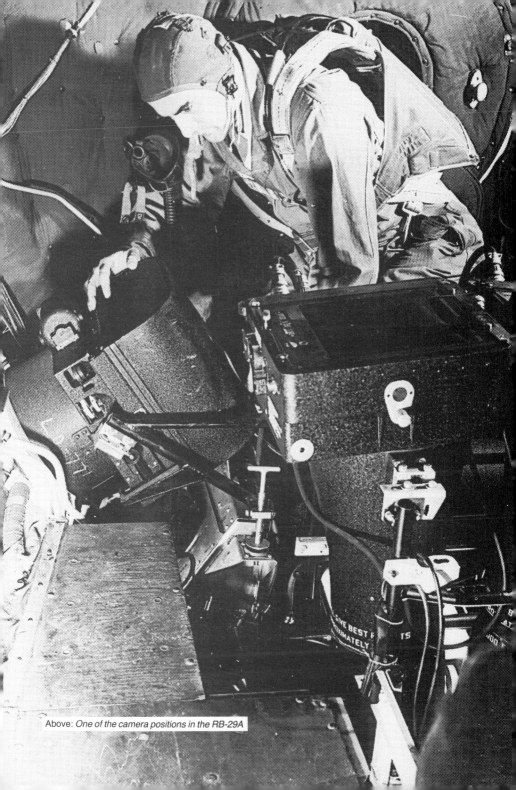

Above: *One of the camera positions in the RB-29A*

On the first reconnaissance flight over Tokyo and Yokohama, a F-13 flew unmolested for a number of hours steadily photographing the area. Local fighters made many attempts to intercept but they were unable to climb to 32,500 feet, the operating height of the F-13. Two F-13s flew over Hiroshima four hours after the atom bomb strike on August 6th, 1945 and again on the 9th after the Nagasaki bomb.

The most important project in which the F-13s were engaged in immediately after the war was the atomic bomb tests at Bikini Atoll in July 1946. Over Exposed played an important role in those tests.

Eight F-13s were used in the project, which was code named "Operation Crossroads" and '1999' was one of the eight. Along with the others Over Exposed was equipped, as were the other F-13s, with 25 cameras.

The aircraft 44-61999 had been built at Renton, Washington and handed over one month before the war ended. For Operation Crossroads it bristled with cameras, all five turrets had them installed.

In June 1946 the F-13s left the States

Below: *One of the stripped down engines as it appears today. The author is seen here laying a wreath in memory of the airmen who lost their lives.*

for Kwajalein Atoll in the Marshall Islands. The tail fins bore a 10 foot black square with the letter 'F' in yellow upon them. A two foot band of yellow was painted just aft of the national insignia, with similiar bands painted towards the wing tips. Behind the yellow tail-band the last three digits of the serial number were painted each side of the fuselage in large black numerals. The last four digits were painted each side of the nose.

Operation Crossroads involved the exploding of two nuclear bombs, one timed to explode several hundred feet above Bikini Atoll's lagoon — 'Able Day' bomb scheduled for July 1st, 1946. 'Baker Day' bomb was to be exploded underwater.

The role of 1999 Over Exposed in the atom bomb tests was to photograph the bombing aircraft as the device left the bomb bay. The other F-13s were to circle the mushroom cloud taking pictures.

On 'Able Day' Over Exposed took off from Kwajalein accompanying B-29 Dave's Dream, which was carrying the bomb, it was 5.25 am. Over the target, Bikini Atoll lagoon, the bomb was released and plunged towards the target ship Nevada. Immediately Over Exposed with cameras rolling dived 1,000 feet and was seven miles away when the air detonation occured.

On the 25th once again Over Exposed was busy, this time filming the results of the under water explosion, as the device had been placed on the sea bed.

With the completion of Operation Crossroads the eight F-13s were relieved of their extra cameras at Wright Field and then they flew on to Roswell Field for screening for contamination. Once cleared they returned to their squadrons.

Over Exposed met up with Captain Tanner and crew for the clandestine Berlin operation. Shortly after this the aircraft and crew came to grief, as so many had before, on the Dark Peak mountains of Derbyshire.

Botha W5103, No. 7 Ferry Pilots Pool, on a ferrying flight from Sherburn-in-Elmet to Harwarden, crashed Round Hill, December 10, 1941.

Map reference 110974 • Map key number 4

There had been numerous problems experienced by pilots flying the twin-engined torpedo bomber the Blackburn Botha. Both in production and other test flying work there had been fatal periods of trouble.

The aircraft had been chosen to re-equip Coastal Command prior to outbreak of war in 1939. First deliveries were made to 608 (North Riding) Squadron, based at Thornaby and East Coast convoy escort duties were got underway. It soon became apparent to the crews that the aircraft was totally unsuited to the role. Apart from the reasonable view afforded the pilot, the rest of the crew could barely see out rendering it all but useless for convoy protection and reconnaissance duty.

Contributing to this aircraft's failure in the role for which it was designed and built were its underpowered engines. Rather than the more powerful Bristol Taurus engines, the Botha had to make do with the lesser powered Perseus engines, the Taurus powerplants going to the Bristol Beaufort torpedo bomber. One particular batch of Bothas had problems with the fuel control system. If full take-off power was held too long then the engines would cut out.

Carrying a torpedo and with the fuel tanks loaded (427 gallons) the Botha could barely claw its way into the air. Should one of the engines fail as it got airborne then it would not stay aloft. In the case of engine failure, pilots were directed to jettison fuel immediately.

In war conditions situations arise that call for aircraft to execute steep dives, either to make an attack or avoid enemy action. The Botha's controls became heavy and difficult to manage in a dive and a great deal of force was required to make a recovery. When pulling out of a dive there was a tendency for it to rear

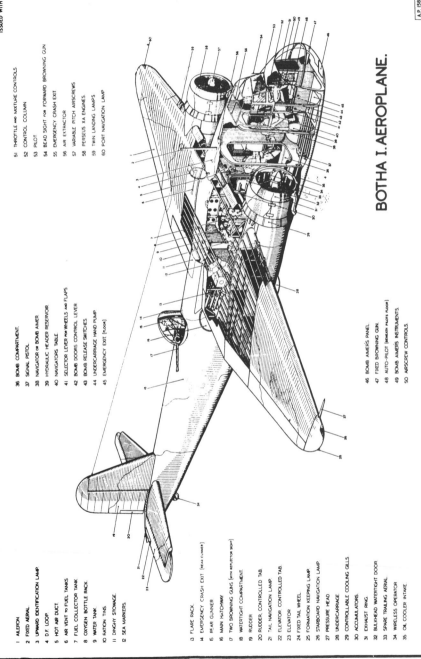

BOTHA I. AEROPLANE.

1 AILERON
2 FIXED AERIAL
3 UPWARD IDENTIFICATION LAMP
4 D.F. LOOP
5 HOT AIR DUCT
6 AIR VENT to FUEL TANKS
7 FUEL COLLECTOR TANK
8 OXYGEN BOTTLE RACK
9 WATER TANK
10 RATION TINS
11 DINGHY STOWAGE
12 SEA MARKERS

13 FLARE RACK
14 EMERGENCY CRASH EXIT (REAR GUNNER)
15 REAR GUNNER
16 MAIN HATCHWAY
17 TWO BROWNING GUNS (WITH REFLECTION SIGHT)
18 WATERTIGHT COMPARTMENT
19 RUDDER
20 RUDDER CONTROLLED TAB
21 TAIL NAVIGATION LAMP
22 ELEVATOR CONTROLLED TAB
23 ELEVATOR
24 FIXED TAIL WHEEL
25 FORMATION KEEPING LAMP
26 STARBOARD NAVIGATION LAMP
27 PRESSURE HEAD
28 UNDERCARRIAGE
29 CONTROLLABLE COOLING GILLS
30 ACCUMULATORS
31 EXHAUST RING
32 BULKHEAD WATERTIGHT DOOR
33 SPARE TRAILING AERIAL
34 WIRELESS OPERATOR
35 OIL COOLER INTAKE

36 BOMB COMPARTMENT.
37 SIGNAL PISTOL
38 NAVIGATOR or BOMB AIMER
39 HYDRAULIC HEADER RESERVOIR
40 NAVIGATOR'S TABLE
41 SELECTOR LEVER for WHEELS and FLAPS
42 BOMB DOORS CONTROL LEVER
43 BOMB RELEASE SWITCHES
44 UNDERCARRIAGE HAND PUMP
45 EMERGENCY EXIT (FLOOR)

46 BOMB AIMER'S PANEL.
47 FIXED BROWNING GUN.
48 AUTO-PILOT (BENEATH PILOT'S FLOOR)
49 BOMB AIMER'S INSTRUMENTS.
50 AIRSCREW CONTROLS

51 THROTTLE and MIXTURE CONTROLS
52 CONTROL COLUMN
53 PILOT
54 BEAD SIGHT for FORWARD BROWNING GUN
55 EMERGENCY CRASH EXIT
56 AIR EXTRACTOR
57 VARIABLE PITCH AIRSCREWS
58 PERSEUS XA ENGINES
59 TWIN LANDING LAMPS
60 PORT NAVIGATION LAMP

A.P. 1588 A, VOL I
FRONTISPIECE

up into a steep climb, whereupon considerable force had to be applied to the controls in order to get the nose down and level. Just taxiing the aeroplane on the ground was far from easy as it would veer first one way then another if the throttles were not handled with great care. Then on take-off the pilot had to be prepared to correct a vicious swing to the right.

Taking all the aircraft's problems into consideration, the Commander-in-Chief Coastal Command sought alternatives to the Botha. In the meantime the faithful Avro Anson was brought back into service for convoy support. However, Blackburn was producing the Botha at a fast rate and attempts were made to find some aspect of service that the aircraft could cope with successfully; among other things, bombing and gunnery training schools and an advanced trainer for Canada and South Africa where air-crews were being trained.

With its firm rejection as an operational 'frontline' aircraft the Botha (580 aircraft in total) was directed to be used as a twin-engined trainer. Despite pleas from Blackburn to be allowed to carry out further modifications, orders were cancelled and production ceased.

In spite of its shortcomings some pilots regarded the Botha as a fairly easy aircraft to fly — if it had little weight to lift off the ground and nothing was demanded of it in the way of aerial manoeuvres.

On Round Hill, by Bleaklow Meadows, just two and a half miles from Woodhead, lie the shattered remains of a Blackburn Botha.

Above: *First Officer T. W. Rogers*

Members of the Air Transport Auxiliary were called upon to ferry all types of aircraft about the country. Aircraft from the United States and Canada arrived at Prestwick and had to be flown to Maintenance Units all over England and Scotland as had aircraft produced in factories in this country. Further ferrying was required between the Mainten-

BEAD SIGHT FOR FIXED GUN
① (OUTSIDE COCKPIT)

② COMPASS

③ STARWHEEL FOR
ADJUSTING
RUDDER BAR

Above: *Botha cockpit*

ance Units and Operational Training Units and Squadrons. Ferry pilots disliked flying the Botha because they had to fly it on their own and there was the very real danger of setting the complicated fuel system (which was positioned well away from the pilot where the wingspar passed through the fuselage), so that the fuel tanks were switched off. A small fuel tank permitted the aircraft to be started up and flown off before running dry, whereupon, with two dead engines the Botha would drop out of the sky.

First Officer Thomas William Rogers of No. 7 Ferry Pilots Pool, Air Transport Auxiliary had been detailed to deliver the aircraft to No. 48 Maintenance Unit at Harwarden, near Chester. From the airfield at Sherburn-in-Elmet to Harwarden was a flight of 90 minutes duration. It was the 10th December, 1941.

Rogers would have gone over the cockpit layout with one of the flight shed engineers at Sherburn. Ferry pilots were called upon to fly aircraft of varying types and so they needed to familiarise themselves constantly with the varying instrument arrangements, also the various snags and peculiarities of the machines they were ordered to deliver.

There were to be no crew or passengers on that delivery flight. Ground crew loaded sandbags into the Botha, these were placed on the seats in the three crew positions to act as ballast, so that the correct trim could be maintained.

The flight was very much routine and ATA pilot Rogers should have arrived at Harwarden about 45 minutes after leaving Sherburn. However, the flight path lay directly across the Dark Peak District.

ATA pilots were forbidden to fly above 5,000 feet and were instructed to fly

Above: *One of the Perseus engines; both engines were recovered by cadets from RAF Henlow*

within sight of the ground, and never at night. These were commonsense instructions because aircraft being ferried rarely carried functioning radios, nor oxygen for altitude flying. The usual method of navigation was to follow railway lines for some of the flight and pick up on landmarks.

For most of the winter days the Peaks, which in places rise to over 2,000 feet, lie shrouded in mist and cloud.

Rogers knew what his estimated time of arrival was, and that after he had climbed above the cloud, how long he must fly in order to clear the Pennines. After 25 minutes flying time he would have estimated that he was over the town of Glossop, clear of the hills and heading towards Stockport.

Perhaps the prevailing westerlies, which had constituted a head wind for the underpowered Botha, had upset his calculations. Whatever the reason, he had decided to drop through the clouds about three minutes before he should have done.

It was a hill sheep farmer who came across the wrecked aircraft the following day. It lay overturned on its back — the pilot was dead, suspended from his seat by his harness.

Rogers was 19 years old, a keen sportsman and point-to-point rider, from Llangadock, Myddfai, Carmarthen. He had been employed at a riding stable near Salisbury when war broke out and he promptly volunteered for the RAF, then a year later was transferred to the ATA.

At the crash site today, 1,750 feet above sea level, lying between Near Black Clough and Middle Black Clough are the remains of the Botha. Large heavy sections of wing give us some idea of the power needed to get the aircraft off the ground — power that was woefully lacking in the Perseus X engines. Those engines were removed in 1968 by RAF officer cadets from Henlow. They had been buried in the peat by the maintenance unit attending the crash.

Below: *A wing section of the Botha; this along with other spars and fragments are all that remain on the surface of the moor.*

Defiant N3378, 255 Squadron, RAF, flying from Turnhouse to Hibaldstow crashed Near Bleaklow Stones, 29th August, 1941.

Map reference 103979 • Map key number 5

No. 255 Squadron was reformed in November, 1940 (it had originally been formed at the end of the First World War) and was stationed at Kirton-in-Lindsey. Its function was to provide protection to the port of Hull which was receiving attention from the Luftwaffe in night raids. During its initial forming period it flew Hurricanes and Spitfires with which the pilots daily practised scrambling to intercept, also circuits and bumps. On the 5th January, 1941, the Squadron went operational with Boulton Paul Defiants.

The Defiant had turned out to be a failure during the Battle of Britain, which had been fought and won some four months earlier, and the type had been switched to various other duties, night fighter operations being one of them. One of the problems of the design was the armament, four machine guns mounted in a power operated turret.

With no forward firing guns the pilot had to think in terms of his gunner's firing arc and position his aircraft accordingly so as to afford his crewman the best possible target. German fighter pilots had quickly discovered the plane's weak spot (below and behind) and the casualties began to mount among the squadrons operating Defiants.

Pilot Officer James Craig, a 24 year old regular officer with plenty of flying experience, was posted to 255 Squadron at its formation. His airgunner, manning the four 303 Browning machine guns, was Bert Hill; his ground crew consisted of two, airframe rigger Johnny Hill and mechanic Rob Robertson, who was a fellow Scotsman. During the months that Hull was being blitzed, Jimmy Craig and his airgunner flew many sorties against the Heinkel 111s and Junkers 88s that nightly bombed the city.

Above: **George Hempstead** seen here lying on the wing of a Spitfire.

Night flying brought casualties to the Squadron, however, balancing this to some degree was the growing number of enemy bombers damaged or destroyed — by the month of June the tally had grown to twelve.

It was whilst the blitzing of British cities was at its worst that the mechanic, Rob Robertson, received a special favour from his pilot, Jimmy Craig. Rob had not received a letter from his wife for a number of days and with the bombing of Lancashire cities he was more than a little concerned — and it showed. Craig noticed his mechanic's glum face and inquired the reason why. At once Craig arranged for Rob Robertson to make a 'flying visit'. He suggested that his mechanic see to his duties early the next day, he would then test fly the aircraft immediately and if the flight path should take them over Warrington and the airfield at Burtonwood, then so much the better.

Others arranged to cover for his duties and Rob Robertson eased his six foot frame into the gun turret of the Defiant and tried to look as if he had every right to be there. It was Rob's first ever flight and it didn't seem long before Jimmy Craig was speaking to the controllers at Burtonwood. Over the intercom Rob asked his pilot to drop him off out of sight of the control tower. The Defiant landed and continued down to the end of the runway and the airfield perimeter where Rob was able to scramble out and hop over the fence. His home was a twenty minute walk and as he set off, he watched as the Defiant climbed away observing the waggling of the wings as Craig bid him farewell.

Two days later Rob arrived back at Hibaldstow to the wrath of his sergeant, who despite not being informed of the absence without leave, had marked him present. Jimmy Craig was more than ready to help the ground crew with lifts to various parts of the country as and when the need arose.

It was around that time that the Squadron began a period of conversion to Beaufighters and during the month of August it was stood down, becoming non operational on the 23rd of that month. Many men were given leave and Rob Robertson went up to Edinburgh to visit his parents. As the time came for him to return he considered ringing up his pilot Jimmy Craig and asking if, by any chance, he was likely to be in Scotland visiting his parents, as he also was a native of the area. In the event he decided against it and returned to Hibaldstow by train.

Upon his return he was distressed to learn that Jimmy Craig had gone missing, flying back from Turnhouse near Edinburgh, to base. On that occasion also, he had been giving one of the ground crew a lift. Aircraftman George Daniel Hempstead, who was a professional golfer at Boston Golf Club,

Boston, in peacetime, had been given a ride — now they were both missing. Squadron Defiants were up, flying along the coast line and out over the water, looking for signs of the missing aircraft and its occupants.

It was almost a month later when two brothers, David and Joe Shepherd, who had a farm in the Glossop area, spotted the wrecked aircraft on the rocky hillside. They had been told that an aircraft had been seen flying low over the hills and had initiated their own search. They found the bodies of the two men seated beside the fuselage; from all appearances they had survived the crash although seriously injured. The pilot had obviously tended to the more seriously hurt passenger, but they had succumbed to the elements and their injuries.

There is some mystery as to exactly what happened — the known facts are, that Defiant N3378 had taken off from RAF Turnhouse, near Edinburgh, at five past eight on Friday morning, 29th August, 1941. Operations personnel at Kirton-in-Lindsey were in contact with the pilot half an hour later. Craig had briefly said over the radio transmitter that he was returning to base, and it was assumed that he was referring to Hibaldstow, but he never appeared. The Defiant should have been over the field at 10.30 am and in one hours time, when there had been no word from Craig, the aircraft was listed as missing and a search was got underway. Visibility was good, except that there was some cloud over the high ground, but N3378 should have been well away from it and in the area of the East Coast.

Why was the pilot so far off his flight path in good flying conditions? Two theories have been suggested — one controversial and, in the opinion of the authors, one more likely to be the case.

After the two bodies had been removed to the Police Station in the town of Glossop, members from No.10 Barrage

Below: *Radiator cowl purporting to show bullet holes.
This piece of wreckage was later removed from the
site.*

Above: *A gulley filled with shattered pieces of fuselage.*

Balloon Unit, based at Middleton, arrived at the scene. It was claimed that they had discovered bullet holes in the wreckage and the theory was put forward that the Defiant had been shot down by a 'friendly' fighter. It was suggested that the incident may have taken place somewhere near Bishop Aukland, halfway along its journey from Scotland — a number of Spitfire squadrons operated in that area. A member of 255 Squadron recalled a rumour that was rife at the time, that a Spitfire had fired on the Defiant causing Craig to turn for base on a wrong heading. If that was the case then Craig, unable or unwilling to return the fire, had taken some evasive action, then dived for home giving out the briefest of messages that he was returning to Hibaldstow.

Another possible reason that might be considered, is that the 24 year old pilot, recently married, had detoured from his flight path in order to fly over the house where his wife was living with her parents. That was Regent House, Belle Vue, in the city of Wakefield — not too great a deviation from the flight path. It was a strong temptation for many pilots flying in this country to pass over their homes — some would even make their presence obvious to their loved ones by circling and making low level passes. Once over the city of Wakefield it was but a short distance, flying time, to the cloud shrouded Pennines.

The mystery of the bullet holes remain unsolved and their existence was denied in an official report of the day — the official comment on the accident stands at: "Aircraft flew into a hillside in low cloud".

Above: *The Defiant's Merlin engine heavily corroded and with every removable part stripped off.*

Blenheim L1476, 64 Squadron, RAF, on a local sector knowledge flight from Church Fenton, crashed Sykes Moor, 30th January 1939.

Map reference 081971 ● Map key number 6

Richard Bridge, aged 23, from the village of Audenshaw, was a member of the Openshaw Out-of-Doors Club and had planned to be out with other club members on a Sunday ramble across the moors. At the start of the hike he was late and so missed his friends: "I decided to follow them and try and catch them up, so I set off to walk from Marple to Woodhead via Chunel as arranged, not knowing that my colleagues had changed their route."

Had Richard Bridge rightly guessed the route taken by the rambling club and followed their tracks, a Blenheim twin engined aircraft of 64 Squadron may have remained undiscovered on Bleaklow for much longer than eleven days.

64 Squadron had been reformed in March 1936 and was delegated as part of the defence of the United Kingdom, moving to Church Fenton, near York in May 1938. The following year, the then much vaunted Bristol Blenheim 1F, a twin engined fighter version of that bomber, was introduced to the squadron. The squadron had begun to concentrate on night flying, so that on the outbreak of the Second World War it would be operational at night only.

On 30th January, 1939, two new squadron members, Pilot Officer Stanley John Daly Robinson and Acting Pilot Officer Jack Elliott Thomas, who had both recently arrived from South Africa, took off from Church Fenton at 9.45 am for a two hour flight — they had been briefed to fly 'local sector knowledge'. Robinson had recently been cleared to fly the Blenheim 1F and could take a passenger; Daly had recently arrived in the squadron and went along rather than the regular airgunner. When they had failed to arrive back at Church Fenton and their estimated time of arrival had long passed, a search was got underway.

Reports had been received that a twin engined aircraft, apparently in trouble, was observed to be descending over the sea close to the town of Withernsea. An observer reported that the aircraft was descending towards the water at an angle of 45 degrees. It was that report which caused the air searches to be made

Above: *Blenheim Mk1, interior of cockpit.*

over the sea rather than the high ground in central England. Eventually the air search was called off on February 9th and the two men were officially listed as 'missing'.

The shattered remains of Blenheim L1476 could well have remained undiscovered for many months, perhaps years, had it not been for that turn of events on that Sunday morning the 11th February.

It was early afternoon when the lone hiker, Richard Bridge, began crossing the desolate moor towards Torside. He came to a large rock and stopped for a rest and a bite to eat. From the rock where he was sitting he scoured the moor looking for signs of life, some indication that his friends were ahead of him. At one point he even thought that he heard the sound of a whistle being blown (a whistle was carried by every member of the walking club) but apart for the odd hare in its winter coat, he saw no sign of human life. As he viewed the landscape from his vantage point at the rock he suddenly caught sight of what appeared to be a tent, billowing in

Below: *As the wrecked Blenheim appeared to Richard Bridge when he discovered it.*

the wind, about a mile away. It struck him as peculiar that anyone would be camping out in the middle of winter on an exposed moor, so he decided to go across and have a look.

After first crossing a stream and then negotiating a swampy area, he began scrambling up a steep, peat covered slope. He remembers wondering to himself what sort of a reception he might expect from the hardy campers — would they consider him to be some sort of a snooper? He continued his climb until he reached the top of the hill where the ground flattened out onto Sykes Moor.

He stopped in his tracks at the sight which met his eyes; for a good distance the ground was littered with jagged metal. A large crater had been torn into the moorland and the broken remains of a tail section jutted into the sky, loose metal panels flapped in the wind. On the tail's rudder was the number L1476 still plainly to be seen.

Wreckage was strewn around over a distance of two acres, and one mud caked engine was lying about one hundred yards from the impact crater. Walking on, not too far distant from the engine, he came upon the limbless and headless torso of a human being. He continued warily among the metal fragments and was sickened to come across other human remains. It seemed to him that arms and legs were everywhere, causing him to wonder at the number of persons involved in the accident. The parachute, that he had mistaken for a tent, was some 600 yards from the impact point and attached to it was a badly mangled body. He turned and ran off, sick with horror, until he reached a path that led down off the moor to a lonely farm called The Reaps some two miles distant, and near to a level crossing at Torside.

There was no telephone at the farm and the farmer, Bert Crossland, directed him to a level crossing and Torside signal box. It was from there that the signalman put a telegraph message through to the railway controller at Manchester, who then in turn contacted Glossop Borough police — by that time it was around 4 o'clock in the afternoon.

Glossop Borough ambulance arrived at Reaps Farm along with some police

Below: *Squadron Leader Heber-Percy and a local police sergeant at the crash scene.*

constables. Constables Clarke, Pearson and Tricket, along with Chief Borough Engineer Roe set off for the wreck guided by Richard Bridge and the farmer, Bert Crossland. They arrived at the site at 5.25 pm, but due to failing light, it was decided to leave the stretchers there and to return the following morning.

9 am Monday morning and a large crowd was gathered at Reaps Farm ready for the journey up onto the moor and the recovery of the remains of the crew. Amongst them was an RAF team from Church Fenton led by Squadron Leader Heber-Percy, also RAF personnel who would act as guards at the site. Two investigation officers from the Air Ministry were also amongst the party as it started out. At the site gamekeepers and landowners joined the group and the ground was scoured for human remains. When these had been gathered up and placed on the stretchers the group set off back down the moor with the grim loads, leaving some RAF personnel as guards

against souvenir hunters and sightseers. There was nothing worth salvaging from the wreckage and members of a digging party made attempts to bury what they could of the remains of L1476.

At Glossop mortuary attempts were made to identify the pieces and from clothing labels it was ascertained that the men were, indeed the missing Pilot Officers. The Deputy Coroner, Mr G. H. Wilson presided at an inquest at Glossop Police Station, where Squadron Leader Heber-Percy was unable to suggest any reason as to why the accident had occured. A verdict of 'death by misadventure' was recorded. Further, it was concluded that the fuel tanks must have exploded upon impact and that was the reason for the wide scattering of wreckage.

With the crash of the Blenheim at the beginning of 1939 the tally of warplanes destroyed in the Peak District began, as the war further intensified air traffic over the high ground.

Above: *One of the engines as it was in the early seventies, and the same engine ten years later. Three of the four 'pots' have been removed by determined souvenir hunters.*

Above: A good will visit to the United States in 1947 by 35 Squadron RAF. One of the Lancasters in this line-up is PA411. Upon its return to this country it was transfered to 230 OCU and crashed at Tintwistle a few months later.

Lancaster PA411, 230 Operational Conversion Unit, on a training flight from Lindholme, crashed Rhodes Hill, December 20th, 1948.

Map reference 034993 • Map key number 7

On the train back to Lindholme in Lincolnshire, Richard Henry Walker opened the 'Daily Herald' and sure enough there it was — a report on the accident. He had heard that his crew had perished in an air crash, but he had hoped that there had been some mistake. There it was in print and there were no survivors — it was his own crew. Lancaster PA411 had flown into a hillside in Derbyshire and all those aboard had perished. His eyes ran over the crew list again and again, there could be no mistake, the names were those of his friends.

There was his pilot, the skipper, Flight Sergeant Jack Sherwood Thompson; navigator, Flight Lieutenant Peter Maskell; signaller, Flight Sergeant Robert Smith; engineer, Flight Sergeant Vincent Graham and signaller, Sergeant William Love. The training personnel on the fatal flight were Flight Lieutenant Thomas Iowerth Johnson, who was the pilot instructor and Flight Sergeant David Harris, who was the engineer instructor.

The reason why Flight Sergeant Richard 'Dick' Walker was not on that fatal flight was because he was on his honeymoon. He had been married the previous week at Fleetwood and all the members of the crew had been in attendance. Immediately after the wedding the crew had returned to Lindholme and continued with their training. It was the second occasion in three years that Dick Walker had escaped death along with his crew.

Dick had joined the RAF too late to take extensive training to become a pilot and see active service, so he did the next best thing and volunteered as an air gunner. He was the youngest of three brothers, his eldest brother was a bomber pilot and survived the war. His

Above: **Sergeant Dick Walker** who missed two fatal flights during his career in the RAF.

other brother had been killed when his aircraft failed to return from the first 1,000 bomber raid on Dusseldorf. He was influenced by their example and expressed a desire to get into the action before the war ended. By the Summer of 1944 when Dick joined the RAF, the invasion of Europe had taken place and it was only a matter of time before Hitler's Germany was defeated.

After training at No.10 Air Gunners School, Walney Island, flying Avro Ansons, he went on to No.21 Operations training Unit at Enstone, where he was crewed up with skipper, Pilot Officer Sisley, an Australian. Then with a complete crew he went on to 1658 Heavy Conversion Unit at Riccall Common and from there to 640 Squadron, which was flying Halifaxes, based at Leconfield.

After flying a number of operations with his new crew, Dick Walker was hospitalised for a short while. It was whilst he was in his sick bed in February 1945, that his crew took off with a full bomb load for a raid on Germany. Pilot Officer Sisley lifted the Halifax from the runway and what all pilots dreaded at that critical point occurred, one of the four engines suddenly failed. With insufficient forward momentum to stay in the air, the Australian dropped the nose of the Halifax and sought to put the bomber down, but they had passed the runway boundary. Upon impact with the ground the rear turret and its occupant were jolted away and the aircraft, with full fuel tanks and bomb exploded.

Sergeant Whitmee's usual position was mid-upper gunner, but with the usual rear gunner, Dick Walker, being in hospital he had changed positions and had been flung away from the doomed bomber along with the rear turret and sustained only minor injuries. Three years later Whitmee was Dick Walker's best man.

Dick Walker finished the war flying 14 operations with another crew, skipper Flight Sergeant Lee. With the end of hostilities in Europe Dick trained as an air traffic controller, but decided to leave the service when the first opportunity came along. However, when the time came around for him to leave the RAF he held a 'demob' party and when he awoke the next day with a hangover, he discovered that somehow he had signed on for another three years. He then took an armourer fitter's course at Kirkham near Blackpool, where he met his future wife.

On October 14th, 1948, he went on to join another crew at 230 Operational Training Unit based at Lindholme. The aircraft were white painted Lancasters and his new skipper was Jack Thompson from Hull. Once again Dick took his crew position as 'tail end Charlie'. Over

Above: *Pilot Officer Sisley (seated centre) Australian pilot of Dick Walker's previous crew. Dick Walker is standing behind his pilot. Only the rear gunner Sergeant Whitmee, survived the crash (seen here standing to Dick Walker's right).*

the nine weeks that followed he flew on nine training trips with his crew, the last one being on December 9th, 1948, just prior to his wedding — suddenly they were all dead, wiped out.

Upon arriving back at Lindholme he was officially informed of the accident and ordered to travel to Hollingworth to identify the bodies of the crew.

Lancaster PA411 had been on a night training flight with two instructors on board. The time of the crash was officially given as ten seconds to midnight; that was arrived at by the shattered wrist watch of the airman who had occupied the rear turret (likely to have been Sergeant Love). Apparently, Flight Sergeant Thompson, began a descent when uncertain of his position, not realising that he was in an area of high ground. He was receiving a strong signal from base and believed that he was much closer than he actually was.

First to reach the burning wreck was Mr John Bagshaw of Old Road, Tintwhistle, and his four sons, Jack (21), Basil (17), Neville (14) and Ernest (12). They had been in bed when they had heard the aircraft low overhead — then there had been a dull bang. Looking out from their windows they could see the sky lit by an orange glow over in the east in the direction of the high ground. It took them just over 30 minutes to reach the site having scrambled up the moor towards the glow of the fire. The first object that loomed up out of the darkness was the tail unit of the Lancaster, still complete with rear turret. A short distance from the rear gun turret was the form of its former occupant.

"One member of the crew, I think he would be the rear gunner, was breathing faintly as he lay near the tail, which was a long way from the body of the flames. I wiped his mouth but sadly he never

This page and opposite: *Photographs taken at the crash scene the following day.*

recovered." Mr Bagshaw later told a reporter of the 'Glossop Chronicle'.

By the time that ambulance, police, and members of the RAF Mountain Rescue Team arrived, Mr Bagshaw and his sons had located three other bodies close by the wreckage. Of the seven bodies subsequently found only two were badly burnt. It was decided that nothing could be done until dawn to remove the bodies from the moor to the ambulances waiting on the Woodhead road. Jeeps drove up as far as they could along a rough track and the stretchers were carried down to them at dawn.

Twelve hours after the crash and smoke was still swirling up from the wreckage. The four Rolls Royce engines had smashed to pieces and the fuselage was ripped to shreds. Odd belongings such as a pen knife, bunch of keys etc, were still being found by the locals long after the main rescue parties had gone.

On January 10th, 1949, Dick Walker was assigned to another crew and was posted to 101 Squadron flying Lincolns at Binbrook. Part of the squadron's duties was to patrol over the North Cape and collect air samples to check for radiation. The Russians were test firing nuclear devices and the Lincoln crews were ordered to fly from sea level to 24,000 feet for periods of eight hours at a time. In January 1951 Richard Walker left the RAF.

Chipmunk WB579, No.2 Reserve Flying School, on a training flight from Barton, crashed Arnfield Moor, July 3rd, 1951.

Map reference 031001 ● Map key number 8

A thick mist covered the moors above Tintwistle, obscuring the rising ground from the sight of the 24 year old pilot of the Chipmunk trainer. Harry Bate Wright was an RAF Volunteer Reserve Pilot, and the flight from Barton and return should have been pretty much routine. However, the weather over Derbyshire and the western side of the Pennines was appalling as Wright let down through the mist and rain.

Suddenly the fixed undercarriage of the Chipmunk struck the ground and the aircraft somersaulted into the peat ridden slopes breaking its back. The pilot managed to dig himself free and stagger off down the moor ending up at Arnfield Farm.

Mrs Thompson, who resided at the farm, was just clearing away the tea things when an urgent knock sounded on the door:

"This man just flopped in, he was covered head to foot in peat and dirt."

Mrs Thompson later told the Glossop Chronicle reporter, "It was difficult to tell if he was in uniform, or what he was wearing."

Harry Bate Wright was suffering from shock and had been trapped in his cockpit for some time, hanging from his straps. He told them at the farm how it had seemed as though he had been trapped for hours caught up in his harness and hanging upside down; it had taken him ages to dig himself out with his bare hands. Fortunately the Chipmunk did not catch fire and Wright suffered no injuries apart from shock. The smell of aviation fuel leaking from ruptured tanks into the ground all around him had helped to spur him on in his attempts to break free.

Police arrived from Stalybridge and Mottram and they split up in parties to search the moors, which were still shrouded in mist. Also at the time there was a persistent drizzle. They were

unsuccessful in locating the aeroplane and even had difficulty in retaining their own sense of direction in the treacherous conditions, consequently the search was abandoned until the folowing day.

It was 7.30 on the Wednesday morning when local police Sergeant Evans and Co-operation gamekeeper, Mr Garnett reached the site of the accident. Once the mist cleared it could be plainly seen from the road and was a 30 minute walk up the moor from Arnfield Farm. An RAF contingent arrived from Bowlee arrived later that day to mount guard over the crashed aircraft. The wreckage was chopped up and dragged off the moor. Because of this it is extremely difficult to pinpoint the site with any degree of accuracy today.

Hurricanes PZ851,PZ765 and PZ854, No.11 Pilot Advanced Flying Unit, on a formation training flight from Calveley, crashed Didsbury Intake, 22nd February, 1945.

Map reference 036988 ● Map key number 9

Among the many European escapees who joined the RAF in order to take part in the fight against Germany, were two teenagers from Belgium, E. M. L. Marien and M. A. L. Orban. It was no easy matter to break free from Nazi dominated territory, and although the most direct route lay across the English Channel, those who were the most successful in their escape attempts usually travelled overland via France, Spain and then either passing through Portugal or Gibraltar.

Both Marien and Orban had been detained for a while in the notorious prison camp of Miranda, in neutral Spain. Upon their being released, possibly brought about because they looked young enough not to cause problems for the Fascist state of General Franco, they made their way to Britain by way of Gibraltar. They reached this country in 1942 and promptly joined the Belgian section of the Royal Air Force at Goring-on-Thames, in the county of Berkshire. Because of some flying experience as a student, pre-war, Orban

was promoted to the rank of Flight Sergeant. Among the group of Belgians taken into the RAF around that time were two brothers who had also fled from the Nazis, they were Jan and Maurice van Risseghem. Their escape through France had been fraught with danger and the account of these two reads like an adventure story.

It had taken the boys two years to reach England, they had been 14 and 17 years of age when they had begun their journey during the German invasion of the Low Countries in May 1940. When France fell the brothers kept on the run, hiding by day and travelling by night. At one point Jan became involved with the Red Cross and whilst he was driving an ambulance for them, and carrying a number of wounded at the time, the vehicle was straffed by low flying German fighters. Jan was wounded and from that day he vowed revenge against the Luftwaffe for firing on a plainly marked vehicle of mercy. He and his brother were hidden by nuns and even Jews; travelled with the Maquis across

Above: *One of the Belgian pilots, Van Risseghem, training in a Harvard.*

France during the nights and, once safely in this country, made it known that they wished to become fighter pilots.

As part of their training, the four young Belgians were sent to London to learn practical English via BBC shows, cinema, dancing and parties. They were expected to become a part of the live audience for such popular radio comedy programmes as ITMA (It's That Man Again) starring Tommy Handley. They

Below: *Training School at Scarborough.*

Above: Training School, Scarborough, Marien is standing fifth from left, third row. Orban is at the front, seated on the grass, third from the right.

found that particular brand of British humour to be all rather mysterious. From London, in the January of 1943, they were sent to Scarborough and from there to Sywell where they were graded — they were well on their way to fulfilling their ambitions to become fighter pilots. They all flew solo for the first time.

From Manchester they travelled to Monkton in Canada to an Elementary Flying Training School (EFTS). In January of the following year they received their coveted pilot's wings and promotion to Flight Sergeants. They returned to England where at last there would be an opportunity to get into the action. Marien and Orban were posted to No.11 Pilot Advanced Flying Unit at Wrexham, where night flying was practised. After 50 hours flying time on Harvards they were posted to Calveley where they were at last given a fighter to train in — the Hurricane.

No.11 PAFU had gone over to training fighter pilots in December 1944 after giving up its twin-engined trainers. The tremendous amount of flying carried out from Calveley can be imagined when it is considered that the PAFU operated

with an establishment of 58 Harvards and 39 Hurricanes. The RAF personnel responsible for training were processing some 250 pilots through the system by 1945. It was an eight weeks course in winter and a six weeks course in summer, each pilot being given 40 hours flying time. Two thirds of the pilots were to be fed to the Special Typhoon/Tempest Operation Training Units, with the remainder of the pilots going to normal Advanced Flying Units — from these to front line squadrons. The war in Europe seemed to be heading towards a climax, with the defeat of Germany sure, the four Belgians were eager for their training to come to completion before the war ended.

It was during the final stages of their training as fighter pilots that two Belgians, Marien and Orban, along with a third, a British trainee pilot called Robinson, died in a multiple crash.

It was the morning of February 25th, 1945 when three Hurricanes took off to practice formation flying. "Stardust" Marien was leading the flight on that occasion. He had earned his nickname because of his obsession with the dance tune of that name; when he wasn't playing the record he was whistling or humming the tune.

Also flying that morning was fellow Belgian Jan van Risseghem, but he was in a Harvard and flying in a different area. Along with his instructor, he landed and learnt that three Calveley Hurricanes had flown into the ground near Tintwistle, at the start of Longendale Valley. Upon learning that Marien and Orban were involved he, along with his instructor, flew over the area in an attempt to locate the crash site, but low cloud prevented a sighting.

We dare not let down through the clouds to investigate, and presumed that Marien had led the other two down through the overcast and into the hill. We flew two more sorties that morning before the cloud cleared for us to see the wreckage, and that would have been around lunchtime."

The accident was a severe blow to many of the pilots and instructors of No.11 PAFU. They were used to fatal accidents, but it seemed all the more tragic when it was considered how the two Belgian lads had escaped from the Germans, only to suffer in a Spanish detainment camp, eventually to arrive in England where they had joined the RAF, almost finish their training as fighter pilots only to die in flying accident.

It had taken two years of training to get them to the stage where they could fly operationally against the Germans. Both Marien and Orban could have got into the fighting much sooner if they had volunteered for Bomber Command, but like their friends, Maurice and Jan Risseghem, they wished to get back at the enemy man to man. Jan had never forgotten the attacks on the plainly marked Red Cross ambulance by the German fighters along the roads of Northern France. He wanted to pay the Luftwaffe back, rather than drop bombs on the inhabitants of German cities.

The war in Europe had only weeks left to run and with the wind-down of the RAF, all flying at Calveley ceased on May 31st, 1945 and the PAFU was disbanded.

Apart from a few scraps of metal scattered around, nothing remains at the site, although a large rock bears the scars of the impact of one of the Hurricane fighters. The bulk of the wreckage was removed at the time.

On several days prior to the tragedy three Hurricanes had been flying up and down Longendale Valley and had been observed to fly under high tension wires strung between pylons. Whether or not they were the same three pilots who had eventually crashed is not known, but the impact point is close to where pylons used to stand before being dismantled.

Above: *A P38J with a collapsed undercarriage — its serial number is a few digits removed from the one which crashed at Tintwistle and is of the same production batch.*

Lightning P38J, 42-67207, HQ Squadron, 554 Fighter Training Squadron, 496 Fighter Training Group USAAF on a training flight from Gox Hill, crashed May 10th, 1944.

Map reference 033997 • Map key number 10

Flight Officer Hugh Allen Jones took off from Goxhill, the American fighter training field near Hull at around 10 o'clock in the morning to carry out a cine-gun, single engine navigation mission. Immediately after take off things went wrong for Flight Officer Jones, he was unable to locate his section — the other three P38s had just disappeared.

However, there was another section that had just got airborne and he was directed to join them as they were also on a navigation flight. The four twin boom fighters set course 270 degrees flying westward and in less than 30 minutes they were over the Pennines. As the high ground loomed up the fighters ran into a cloud bank, whereupon a left turn of 180 degrees was made. The aircraft were in the clouds for about 30 seconds and upon clearing them, Flying Officer Jones's aircraft was missing from the formation, where he had been flying in the number two position. Upon the section's return to Goxhill the aircraft was reported as missing which, had

occured when the section made the turn whilst in cloud.

Reports of a crashed aircraft came in and a USAAF investigating officer flew to Ringway where the RAF engineering

Below: *Flight Officer Hugh Jones*

officer, Flying Officer Rowbotham was able to report what his team had found.

That officer reported that they had discovered the wrecked P38 scattered over an area about one hundred yards by fifty yards. It was thought that the aircraft had gone into the ground inverted and upon impact had burst into flames. The hillside upon which the aircraft had crashed was 1000 feet above the surrounding area. The official report stated that there were no witnesses to the accident, however, a sheep farmer gathering some of his flock, reported seeing the fighter heading towards the moors with thick smoke pouring from one of the engines.

Jones had flown a total of 300 hours on the P38, 17 hours on the J version and so was familiar with the type. At the time of his disappearance the section were flying at a height of 5000 feet and so were well above the hills in that area. Rather than him flying into the hill as so many aircraft had done before, and would do after, it would seem that he had become disoriented in cloud whilst flying on one engine. It had occured when he was out of visual contact with the other aircraft during those vital 30 seconds in the clouds.

Meteors WA971 and VZ518, 66 Squadron, RAF on a training flight from Linton-on-Ouse, crashed Sliddens Moss, April 12th, 1951.

Map reference 069029 • Map key number 11

The Commander of 'A' Flight, Flight Lieutenant Bill Howard, DFC authorised a training flight of four aircraft, they were to be led by Flight Lieutenant David Merryweather Leach. The pilots were instructed to climb to 30,000 feet and practice cine gun attacks — two aircraft versus the other pair; the flight was scheduled to take one hour fifteen minutes. The met. forecast was 8/8ths cloud cover from approximately 1,500 feet to 20,000 feet.

The purpose of the exercise was for the aircraft to make a snake climb to the specified height whereupon one pair would make a cine gun attack on the other two Meteors.

It was Thursday, April 12th, 1951, at 9.15 in the morning when two Meteors took off, to be followed ten seconds later by the second pair. Taking off with Leach as his number two was Flying Officer Tony Hauxwell; leading the

second pair was Flying Officer Leslie Hayward. He recalled the events that led to disaster for two of the Meteors.

"We entered cloud at about 300 feet and then climbed in a south westerly direction. At 30,000 feet we were still in cloud."

Standard procedure for carrying out formation flying through cloud was for both number one and number three, leader of each pair to fly at a steady, constant speed with the throttle open at a specified setting.

At that point David Leach radioed back to Linton-on-Ouse that cloud extended as high as 30,000 feet and that he considered it unsuitable for the exercise. He then informed them that he intended to return to base immediately. He mentioned that they would practise instrument flying and GLA approaches on the way back. Leach spoke to the others over the R/T and told them that

Above: *Members of 66 Squadron at Linton; second from right front row is David Leach and third from right is Leslie Hayward.*

he was descending to 20,000 feet. Once at that height he again spoke to the other three informing them of his

Below: *Tony Hauxwell*

intentions. All they had to do was to follow him home.

"He called to us that he was turning on a reciprocal course and heading back for base. Ten seconds later I also turned onto a reciprocal course.

"Shortly after that David called that he could see Leeds through a hole in the cloud and that he and Tony were going down.

"I called back that myself and my number two were still in cloud and that we would be staying at 20,000 feet until I could be sure of our position.

"Some five minutes later I called David and did not get a response. Having called several more times and still not receiving an answer I contacted Northern Radar and asked them to try and get in touch with him. They called several times also without success. At that point I instructed my number two to return to base and remained airborne another ten minutes trying to raise the other two — having no success I returned to base."

Unfortunately, David Leach had made a basic navigational error in that the climb out from Linton had covered approximately 80 miles and the descent would only cover half that distance putting his position still over the Pennines. On the descent the leader of the second pair, Flying Officer Hayward, felt uneasy and never dropped below 10,000 feet in that area.

It would seem likely that the built up area David Leach had mistaken for Leeds, was in fact Stockport.

The two aircraft must have levelled out and flown into the ground at 9.45 am. The weather was bad and the hills covered in cloud. Later that afternoon, Leslie Hayward took up an Airspeed Oxford with several members of the squadron on board, and flew over the hills and along the approximate flight path. Wreckage was eventually spotted about three miles from Holme Moss television mast.

Mountain Rescue teams attempted to find the crash site but the deteriorating weather conditions and failing light thwarted their efforts. On the following morning Friday, 13th the ground search was resumed but in a blinding rain storm and showers of snow. Attempts to reach the site from the Crowden end had to be abandoned as visibility worsened.

A party of three decided to make an attempt from the Holme Moss end. After driving up the Woodhead-Holmfirth road to the television mast, two police constables led by a Manchester Corporation Waterworks Range Warden, Mr

Below: **David Leach** is seen here facing the camera and demonstrating a recent 'bounce', or mimicking the other pilot who is in mid explanation.

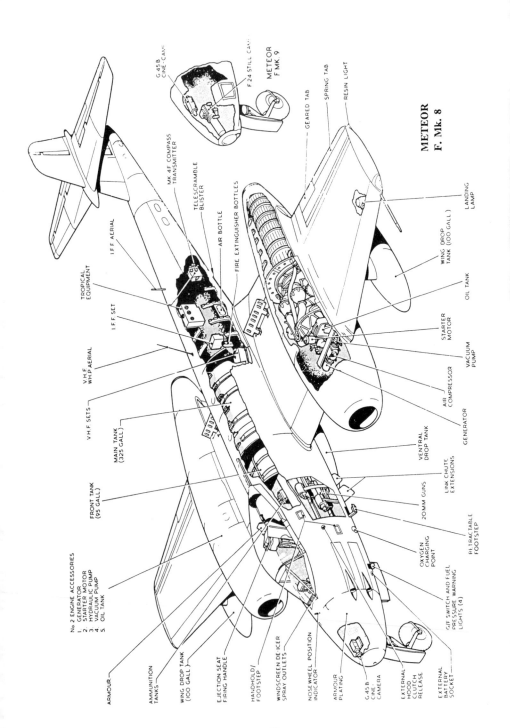

G 45 B CINE-CAM...

F 24 STILL CAM...

METEOR
F MK. 9

GEARED TAB

SPRING TAB

RESIN LIGHT

MK 4F COMPASS TRANSMITTER

TELESCRAMBLE BLISTER

AIR BOTTLE

FIRE EXTINGUISHER BOTTLES

I F F AERIAL

LANDING LAMP

WING DROP TANK (100 GALL)

TROPICAL EQUIPMENT

OIL TANK

I F F SET

STARTER MOTOR

VACUUM PUMP

V H F WH P AERIAL

AIR COMPRESSOR

GENERATOR

V H F SETS

MAIN TANK (325 GALL)

VENTRAL DROP TANK

FRONT TANK (95 GALL)

LINK CHUTE EXTENSIONS

20MM GUNS

No 2 ENGINE ACCESSORIES
1 GENERATOR
2 STARTER MOTOR
3 HYDRAULIC PUMP
4 VACUUM PUMP
5 OIL TANK

RETRACTABLE FOOTSTEP

OXYGEN CHARGING POINT

ARMOUR

AMMUNITION TANKS

WING DROP TANK (100 GALL)

EJECTION SEAT FIRING HANDLE

HANDHOLD/ FOOTSTEP

WINDSCREEN DE-ICER SPRAY OUTLETS

NOSEWHEEL POSITION INDICATOR

ARMOUR PLATING

G 45 B CINE-CAMERA

EXTERNAL HOOD CLUTCH RELEASE

EXTERNAL BATTERY SOCKET

G/F SWITCH AND FUEL PRESSURE WARNING LIGHTS (4)

METEOR
F. Mk. 8

Tom Fazackerley, cut across peat bogs of Tooleyshaw Moss and onto Sliddens Moss. After they had covered about two miles they came across the first piece of wreckage — it was 1.30 pm. Scattered across Sliddens Moss for as far as they could see were lumps of wreckage. The bodies of the two pilots, Leach and Hauxwell lay 150 yards apart.

Flight Lieutenant David Leach was 26 years old when he died; he was married and lived at Skelton Grange, York. He was flying WA 791 and had flown a total of 731 hours, 155 hours on Meteors — an experienced pilot.

Flying VZ 518, was Flying Officer Anthony Hauxwell, aged 25, with a total of 378 hours flying time and 186 of them on the type. He was also married and lived at Skelton Grange.

At the inquest held at Stalybridge Town Hall in May, 1951, the coroner, Mr P. F. Fearns, after hearing the evidence, declared that he was convinced that the planes flew into the ground and the jury returned a verdict of "Misadventure due to the planes hitting the ground owing to poor flying conditions."

Sabre F86E, 19234, 137 (T) Flight RCAF, on a test flight from Ringway, crashed Black Hill, Holme Moss, December 14th, 1954.

Map reference 091051 • Map key number 12

As darkness was falling on Tuesday, December 14th, 1954, a single engined jet fighter tore down Holme Valley passing low over the village of Holme. A number of inhabitants of Holmfirth and the village of Holme saw the aircraft fly towards the high ground near Holme Moss television mast. As it disappeared from sight over the brow of the hill there was a tremendous bang and the darkening sky was lit by an orange glow.

Within minutes the police had been notified and shortly afterwards the local fire engine and other vehicles were climbing up the steep and winding road towards the television mast. The fire engines from Meltham, Marsden and Elland followed later. First onto the moor was the landlord of the Fleece Inn, Mr Harry Shaw; he decided to proceed alone to try and find the crashed plane. Although there was a strong smell of burning in the night air, he was unable to locate the wrecked fighter and, after an hour, he returned to the television station where a large crowd was gathering.

A search party was formed of seven firemen and six policemen, led by gamekeeper Mr Kenneth Tinker of Meltham. As they set off by the light of torches a biting wind lashed them; the moor was covered in drifted snow from a storm of the previous week and the ground was treacherous under foot — visibility was down to a few yards.

Finally the darkness yielded a faint glow and the crashed Sabre, with Royal Canadian Air Force markings, was located. The wings had been torn away by the impact but the fuselage around the cockpit area was intact. Of the pilot there was no sign and at first it was suggested that he might have baled out. However, one of the party pointed to the ejector seat, which was still firmly in position, although the cockpit canopy was shattered. It was obvious that the aircraft's occupant had been catapulted out and must be in the vicinity. A search

59

was instigated around the front of the wrecked plane, but they were only able to find the pilot's helmet. It was decided to try again next morning when it was daylight and they made their way back to the station.

Half an hour after the party arrived back, the RAF Mountain Rescue Team from Harpur Hill, Buxton, turned up and once again, Mr Tinker volunteered to lead another party out to the site of the crash. When they got to the plane they widened out in their search for the missing pilot, reasoning that a man travelling in an aircraft at maybe four to five hundred miles per hour, would continue to do so, even after his machine had come to a dead stop. Sure enough, some 80 yards from the fighter plane they came across the body of the pilot.

As the stretcher party carried the body off the moor winds of up to 60 miles an hour were blowing and rain was lashing the rescuers; visibility was down to a few yards. They were guided back by searchlights at the TV station, these were turned and pointed into the air by the BBC engineers to act as beacons. The dead Canadian pilot, Flying Officer Patrick V. Robinson, aged 28, had only been married a few weeks previously. He was taken to the mortuary at Holme Valley Memorial Hospital.

The crashed fighter was a Canadair built version of the American F86 Sabre. The type was designed and built by North American Aviation of California shortly after the end of the Second World War. With its swept back wings it became the classic fighter of the jet age, and arrived in time to take on the Russian built MIG15 in the Korean War. Canadair of Montreal built upwards of 2,000 Sabres under licence, designated F86Es and went on to supply the sound barrier breaking day fighter to other airforces of NATO countries.

With the 'Cold War' in its infancy, strong defences in Europe were being built up and the North Atlantic Treaty Organisation came into existence — Canada being one of its members. Part of Canada's commitment to the treaty was to European air defence, and for that task the RCAF chose the best fighter in the western world with which to equip its squadrons. Bases were provided in England, France and Germany.

On September 23rd, 1952, Canadian 430 (Silver Falcon) Squadron along with two other squadrons in number 2 Wing, took off from Uplands in Canada and flew in stages via Iceland and Scotland to Grostenquin in France. One of the pilots in 430 Squadron taking part in 'Leapfrog 2' was Pat Robinson. The ferrying operation, in easy stages, took two weeks to reach the base in France.

After many months in the front line squadron in Europe, taking part in exercises and shooting competitions, Pat Robinson was seconded to 137 (T) Flight operating from Ringway.

At various places in England civilian contractors were engaged in extensive refurbishing of both RAF and RCAF Sabres. Former RCAF Sabre 2s were done up at Ringway prior to the aircraft being transferred to Greece and Turkey, whilst Sabre 4s of the RAF were reconditioned and then sent to Italy and the non NATO country of Yugoslavia. The work involved a complete overhaul of both engine and airframe. Everything was removed, dismantled and checked, then new parts were fitted where necessary and modifications made.

Once the overhaul was completed to the satisfaction of the inspectors the test pilots then flew them. It was whilst Sabre F86E, 19234, was being test flown from Ringway by Pat Robinson that it flew into the hillside.

Swordfish P4223, 751 Squadron, Fleet Air Arm, on a ferrying flight, crashed Heydon Head, Holme Moss, January 25th, 1940.

Map reference 085046 • Map key number 13

It looked like a hut in the course of construction to a small group of winter sports enthusiasts, as they viewed the unusual intrusion to the moorland skyline. They had walked to the top of Holme Moss with their skis and from there sped down the hillside to the village of Holme, without investigating or reporting the sighting. It was a fortnight later that a workman decided to take a look at the unfamiliar object.

A Cheshire County Council road man involved in the clearing of snow on the Holme Moss Road, near Woodhead, stood gazing at the object trying to make out what it was. The workman, John Davies decided to make the two mile trek across the frozen moor, and as he drew closer the jumbled shape began to take form.

Scrambling across Heydon Brook he made his way up to, what had turned out to be, a wrecked biplane. The pilot was still strapped in the cockpit, and it looked as though he had been killed instantaneously when the plane had hit the ground. Davies tramped back across the moor and down to Woodhead, about five miles away, to telephone the police.

The Royal Navy Volunteer Reserve Officer, Sub-Lieutenant Gerald Vyvian Williamson, had been reported missing a month earlier on a routine flight. He had become separated from the others in the flight of four Swordfish aircraft of 751 Squadron, on a routine flight heading South. The Fairey Swordfish usually carried a crew of three in an open cockpit, but on that fatal flight there was only the pilot on board.

At the inquest held at Mottram it was stated that Williamson had over ten years flying experience. He had joined the Civil Air Guard in 1938 at its formation on the outbreak of war. From

Above: *Early days when the wreck site was being 'rediscovered' by members of the public. Much has now been cleared by collectors.*

there he volunteered for war service and was posted to the Fleet Air Arm in November, 1939. At the time of his death he was honorary secretary of the Yorkshire Light Aeroplane Club. He had been one of the founder members of that organisation and had been described as one of its best pilots.

The County Pathologist, Dr Grace, who conducted the post-mortem, said that ice had formed in the man's heart and other organs. Death was due to a fracture of the base of the skull and he told the Coroner that death would have been instantaneous. The Coroner went on to record a verdict in accordance with the medical evidence and he further complimented the police and Mr Davies for their work. Mr Williamson left a widow and a six year old son.

A further near tragedy was avoided the following month when a party of

RAF personnel became lost overnight after working at the wreck site.

A sergeant and seven men, based at Holmfirth, had been detailed to go and bury the wreckage. The landlord of the Fleece Inn in the village of Holme, Mr Harry Shaw, offered to act as a guide to the RAF party and drove ahead of them to the top of Holme Moss. The RAF lorry was parked up in an abandoned quarry and Harry Shaw led the team across the moor to the wreck — it was Wednesday, 13th March.

"I guided the men to the plane, promising to come back up for them in the afternoon." Harry Shaw recalled. Returning later in the day, accompanied by a bus conductor friend, Harry could find no sign of the RAF work party. They searched around the area but could not find them. The bus conductor blew constant blasts on a whistle, but as far as they could tell there was no answering call, although there was a strong wind blowing at the time. It was around five o'clock in the afternoon.

The two men returned to the quarry and continued to sound blasts on the lorry's horn, but to no avail. They returned to the village of Holme and raised the alarm. Within a short time police, soldiers, special constables and civilians were scouring the moors and continued to do so through the night.

Just before noon the following day, one of the men amongst the searchers, Mr William Garnett, a Manchester Corporation gamekeeper from the small village of Woodhead spotted the missing men. Earlier he had been told by some of the other searchers, that footprints at the site seemed to indicate that the men may have walked away in a westerly direction. As a consequence of that information William Garnett set off to scour Big Crowden Stream.

"I was walking across the top when I saw a flock of grouse working against the wind. Grouse never work against the wind unless they have been disturbed. As soon as I saw them I knew that the search was coming to an end. True enough, when I looked down the sloping ground I saw black objects moving."

He blew his whistle and waved to the missing men and they returned the wave. Hurrying down to them he found an exhausted bunch of men — they had kept walking all through the night, and had eaten nothing for over twenty four hours. They asked William Garnett to guide them back to the aircraft crash site. He told them that it was out of the question and that they needed food and drink. And that they were much closer to Woodhead and it would be much easier to walk in that direction, than to climb back towards the ground that was the highest point in Cheshire.

He led them off and on the way they came to, what was then, a rifle range

Below: *This engine was reclaimed by cadets from RAF Henlow.*

Above:*Sub Lieutenant Gerald Vyvian Williamson*

direction and when they were eventually found, they were two miles away from the crash site. During the night they must have been walking in vast circles hopelessly lost.

Five days later, six of the men once again returned to the site to complete the job of burying the wreckage. On that occasion they were carrying a Very light pistol. Before setting out in the morning they had arranged that if they were not back by midday, then the landlord of the Fleece Inn, Harry Shaw, would sound the alarm. Ten minutes before noon the lorry rolled up at the Fleece with all of them safely aboard.

Two other men who had shared their grim adventure of the previous week were still in hospital suffering from the effects of exposure.

high up the valley. From there he telephoned the George and Dragon Inn and requested that the landlady, Mrs J. Bagshaw, have some food ready. After rest and something to eat the exhausted men were driven back to the Victoria Hotel, in Holmfirth where they were supplied with a change of clothing.

The danger of treating the moors with a casual indifference is emphasised in this account of the eight RAF men. They were not too great a distance from the road and yet they had lost their way, when they attempted to return to the lorry on their own accord instead of waiting for the guide. They had heard blasts on the whistle, but they had not been able to make their own responses heard because of the high wind. The party had then walked off in the opposite

Liberator B-24H-20 42-94841, 857 Bombardment Squadron, 492 Bombardment Group, USAAF. On a pre-mission training flight, crashed on Twizzle Head Moss, 9th October, 1944

Map reference 103035 ● Map key number 14

It was dubbed a hard luck outfit among the members of the 'Mighty Eighth'. 492 Bomb Group suffered heavily at the hands of the Luftwaffe for the third time in less than eight weeks. Other B24 Liberator Groups that had come into operation at the same time had not so much as seen a German fighter.

The 492 Bombardment Group had moved to North Pickenham, England, in April, 1944 and took part in daylight raids on German industry. After heavy losses, 54 aircraft between May and July, the Group was transferred at the beginning of August to clandestine operations over Occupied Europe. Those covert operations known as 'Carpetbagger' were based at Harrington, Buckinghamshire and involved the dropping of secret agents and supplies to the Resistance.

One of the aircrews involved crashed in bad weather on Twizzle Head Moss, near Holmfirth, whilst on a routine training flight, killing all but one of the nine onboard.

The crew had flown out from Maine in June, just prior to D-Day, arriving at Prestwick. From there they were assigned to 856 Bombardment Squadron, 492 Bombardment Group.

Nose art for their B24 was a packet of Lucky Strike cigarettes. Before every mission the crew, whilst awaiting to board their aircraft, used to smoke a Lucky Strike cigarette by way of a good luck ritual. On one occasion there was no time for them to enact the ritual and, over Hamburg, flak damage was sustained to two engines. The pilot, 2/Lt Pitsenbarger, nursed the bomber back on two engines and one of those was running underpowered because of damage. Fuselage, wings and control surfaces were riddled with holes.

Back over their base at North Pickenham they were given clearance to land immediately. Suddenly another B24 flew close beneath them. Neither crew had seen the other, apparently the other bomber's radio was not functioning.

Lucky Strike's nose dropped down and collided with the other aircraft's tail unit causing it to drop out of the sky and onto the airfield. Only one man survived the impact. Lucky Strike stalled and hit the runway where it skidded along breaking itself in two. The rear gunner was flung out and killed, but the rest of the crew walked away with cuts and bruises. The two pilots, Pitsenbarger and 2/Lt James Nendel both suffered broken noses as

their faces struck the instrument panel.

In September, 1944, the crew took part in transport duties flying fuel and supplies to the Paris area in support of Patton's breakthrough and race to the German border.

On Monday, October 9th, 1944, the crew took off to test fly a recently repaired B-24 in preparation for a mission that night. It also doubled as a training flight for them. They were to fly a circuitous course known as a 'Round Robin' heading north to miss the heavy air traffic over the Midlands. On this occasion they took one of the ground crew along with them, just for the ride, Cpl Clarence Watson.

Their aircraft was not one of the usual B-24s painted all black, but was the standard drab olive green camouflage without markings apart from the national insignia.

Below: *One of the bombers of 857 Squadron, in black paint, used in clandestine operations, code-named 'Carpetbagger'.*

Below: **Elmer D. Pitsenbarger,** pilot.

Above: Crew 3674, official crew photograph taken in front of the B-24 that they were to ferry to Prestwick. Eight of those pictured were involved in the fatal crash.

Back row left to right: J. Bliss, navigator; F. Cser, bombardier; E. Pitsenbarger, pilot; J. Nendel, co-pilot.

Front row left to right: J. W. Zwinge, wireless operator; P. Farris, engineer; C. Anderson, despatcher; C. McQuade, not involved in crash; F. Villelli, ball gunner; H. Stee, not involved in crash.

The crew for the flight was as follows:
Pilot: 1/Lt Elmer D. Pitsenbarger
Co-pilot: 2/Lt James Nendel
Navigator: F/O Jack M. Bliss
Bombardier: F/O Frank Cser
Engineer: T/Sgt Presley S. Farris
W/Operator: T/Sgt Zoe W. Zwinge
Ball Gunner: S/Sgt Frank A. Villelli
Despatcher: S/Sgt Curtis Anderson
Tail Gunner: Cpl Charles T. Lowblad
Passenger: Cpl Clarence Watson

Take-off was at 2.10 in the afternoon from Station 179, Harrington, in poor visibility. Elmer Pitsenbarger (Pits) headed the nose of 841 north flying in low cloud all the way to the Scottish border. The weather worsened and the navigator, Jack Bliss advised his pilots to turn and head for base.

Curtis Anderson was assisting the engineer, Presley Farris, on this trip as he had no agents or supplies to despatch. He was on the flight deck, standing behind Pitsenbarger when he heard the navigator telling Pits that there was some high ground in the area.

At that point Anderson requested permission to move back along the aircraft to his crew position in the waist. Pits gave his OK and Anderson began making his way towards the tail. Forward through the cockpit window they could see nothing as they were flying through wisps of cloud.

Anderson reached the waist position and as he plugged in his intercom he glanced outside and saw green grass flashing beneath the aircraft, then it all went black.

Gradually, Curtis Anderson came to and found himself lying on the ground with his clothes and hair on fire.

Quickly he struggled out of his parachute harness and ripped off his leather jacket. Scooping up handfuls of peat he put out the fire on his head. Riverlets of burning fuel were streaming all around and ammunition was exploding up the moor a little way where the shattered

bomber lay – a blazing inferno.

When he tried to walk he found that he could only manage a few steps before collapsing against a banking.

Out of the mist and smoke two figures appeared and made their way towards him calling out to him as they did so.

When the first two locals reached the scene they asked the deeply shocked crewman his name. He could only reply, "I come from California".

Another crewman had survived the crash, the bombardier, Frank Cser who, like Anderson, had been flung clear. However, his injuries were so severe that he was to die before morning.

One of the first to the accident site was Harold Haigh, a private in the Royal Army Pay Corps. He was on leave and working in his garden at the foot of the hills, in the village of Holme when the American bomber had flown low over the village. It had been low enough for him to make out the markings. He had decided that it would never get over the hills if it didn't gain some height quickly.

He watched it as it passed out of sight, whereupon he distinctly heard a loud thud. Setting off to investigate he met Mr William Battye of Holme Banks, who had also heard the bomber fly over and crash. Together they set off from the road and began the trek across the deep gullies and peat bogs. At first they were unable to locate the aircraft and by that time they had covered about a mile. It was the sound of exploding ammunition that guided them through the mist to the site.

The bomber had bellied in on the moor and scored a huge furrow for a distance of about one hundred yards, disintegrating as it went, before bursting into flames.

William Battye thought that he could see movement in the wrecked fuselage, but the heat was too severe to make a rescue attempt. All they could do was to

Above: *Interior of the B-24; vision forward was poor.*

stand and watch at a safe distance as fuel tanks exploded and bullets sprayed the area. Figures could be seen in the conflagration.

They eventually discovered Curtis Anderson and attempted to lift him so as to carry him off the moor, but that only brought screams of agony. It was later found that his pelvis was broken. They gently laid him down and covered him with his parachute. Although they made him as comfortable as they could, he passed out through the pain he was experiencing in his abdomen.

It was about then that they discovered Pilot Officer Frank Cser, his parachute had opened and was billowing in the wind. There was little that they could do for him as he had suffered massive injuries to his head and was bleeding profusely.

Private Haigh set off back to the road

to fetch help. He managed to get a lift down into Holme where he alerted the Police, Ambulance and Fire services. An earlier attempt by a lady in Holme to alert the rescue services had been dismissed by them. Now they were on the scene two hours after the crash.

When they reached the burning wreck they found both airmen and Mr Battye suffering from exposure.

Harold Haigh had returned to the scene with the rescuers and was able to assist with the carrying of Anderson off the moor by stretcher. Anderson did recover consciousness during that hazardous journey and recalls how Harold Haigh and the three firemen were sinking up to their knees in mud.

Frank Cser was partly carried off in his parachute, and partly strapped to a fireman's ladder.

By the time that the bombardier was

70

Above: *Signs of an intense fire at the crash site; very little remains to be seen apart from the undercarriage legs.*

placed in the ambulance it was dark. The injured men were rushed to Holme Valley Memorial Hospital, Holmfirth.

At 4 am the following morning Frank Cser died from his injuries.

Curtis Anderson had suffered 1st, 2nd, and 3rd degree burns to his face, ears, neck, throat, hands, arm, both legs and right foot, plus a fractured pelvis.

From crashing to arrival at Hospital it had taken three hours hard work.

The pilot and co-pilot, Elmer Pitsenbarger and James Nendel were found burnt and charred, still strapped in their seats on the shattered flight deck. The rest of the crew were found scattered around amongst the wreckage, most were badly burnt and all had suffered servere injuries due to the two hundred plus mph impact.

For a while two crewmen lay undiscovered, then on Tuesday afternoon, Corporal Lowblad's body was found under some previously unchecked wreckage. One man remained unaccounted for until Thursday and it was thought that perhaps he had baled out. Consequently, the moors were searched by police and USAAF personnel for many hours.

A Field Maintenance Group from the 3rd Strategic Air Depot, Watton, arrived on the Thursday to cut up the larger pieces of wreckage with oxy-acetylene torches. As they worked on the port wing human remains were discovered under the port inner engine. They were of a coloured man and were later identified as the remains of Corporal Clarence Watson, the ground crew man who had asked to be taken along just for the ride.

On 3rd January, 1945 Curtis Anderson was flown home. He was finally discharged from hospital in October 1946, after plastic surgery had repaired facial injuries.

Fortress B-17G-65, 43-37667, 709 Bombardment Squadron, 447 Bombardment Group, USAAF. Putting hours on newly fitted engines, crashed Meltham Moor, April 6th, 1945.

Map reference 070098 • Map key number 15

The Second World War had just one month to go before its end, when an American four engined bomber bounced up Meltham Moor breaking the backs of two of the crew, the pilot and navigator. Five of the regular crew members were not along on the flight — the waist, ball and tail gunners were not required. The bombardier, 2/Lt George Kinder, had been ordered to attend a meeting called by the squadron bombardier and so he too missed being involved in the accident.

"If not for that meeting I would have been on board with the crew and more than likely up in my bombardier's position right in the front of the airplane. I would have been thrown out like the other two were, through the Plexiglass nose."

The crew had not been long in this country having received movement orders to proceed overseas at the beginning of February, 1945. Upon arriving in England after sailing across the Atlantic, they were posted to 709 Squadron, 447 Bomb Group, which was stationed at Rattlesden, near Stowmarket, Suffolk. By the time of the accident they had flown six missions over Germany. The day before the accident the pilot, Winston Johnson, and the navigator, Walter Vukelic, had flown their last mission when their Air Division had attacked marshalling yards, ordinance depots and airfields.

The following day, 447 Bomb Group was not required for bombing raids and 709 Squadron were able to catch up on some maintenance. The engine fitters had just finished installing two power plants to Fortress 667 and a crew was needed to take it up to test and run-in the new engines. The aircraft's regular crew were unable to do the test flight and 'Winnie' Johnson volunteered to do the job.

It was 5.10pm Friday 6th April, when the five man crew took off in Fortress 667. At the controls was Winnie Johnson; in the co-pilot's seat was Raymond Parks and between the two pilots was Robert J. Schnug. Schnug would be the busiest member of the crew on that trip, for he had the job of checking cylinder head temperatures and oil pressures of the two new engines. Because they were supposed to be flying locally, the navigator, Walter Vukelic was not required to plot any course and felt very much a passenger. Likewise the radio operator, Robert Woodbeck, considered that he was along for the ride.

Their troubles began when one of the crew suggested that, instead of just stooging around, they could fly up to Manchester (the reason for the suggestion has long been forgotten) and then fly back again. Sadly, Winnie Johnson agreed to the idea and pointed the nose of the aircraft in a north westerly direction.

As they approached the Pennines the weather closed in and they soon began to lose sight of the ground causing them to go on to instrument flying. Johnson nosed the aircraft down gently and hoped for a glimpse of some landmark that would help identify their position but with the cloud ceiling down to about 600 feet and high ground in the area, the situation was becoming more hazardous by the second.

Repeatedly, Johnson asked his navigator, Vukelic for their position and a course for Rattlesden. Vukelic, understandably, was unprepared for the situation they now found themselves in, he had not plotted a course at the outset because there was no need to. In hindsight, perhaps it would have been the

wiser course of action to have gained height, then relied on a fix obtained by the wireless operator. As it was, the crew were completely lost and were still trying to rely upon visual contact with the ground.

Becoming increasingly apprehensive as the daylight diminished and still not receiving a clear course, Johnson told his co-pilot Ray Parks to take over the 'ship' whilst he went down into the nose to assist Vukelic identify their position. As Johnson moved out of his seat, the engineer, Robert Schnug took his place. The bomber was in the hands of the co-pilot which was unauthorised as he had not been cleared to fly unassisted by a pilot, but they were in trouble.

In the nose of the B-17 Vukelic was trying to peer out and orientate himself with the map he held. Johnson ordered him to use the Gee system of navigation and establish their position in that way. Over the intercom he ordered Parks to get some height under the aircraft. At the controls, Ray Parks had the advantage of a windscreen wiper enabling him a clearer view ahead and as he began to pull back on the control column he suddenly saw the ground.

The dark green of the moorland flashed by underneath, and as the angle of the climbing bomber coincided with the upward slope of the ground, contact was made with the heather. Suddenly the ball turret was ripped away as the B-17 smacked onto the moor. Skipping and ripping along at over 150 miles an hour the 17 tons of metal shook off propellors, engines and panels before one of the wings dug into the peat slewing it around to face the way it had come. As the foward motion stopped both Johnson and Vukelic were hurled through the Plexiglass nose and onto the moor.

The other three crew members received only minor injuries and quickly evacuated the plane. Sergeants Wood-

CREW 43 GREEN SQD.

Above: Crew 709, official crew photograph taken shortly after its formation; three of the officers were involved in the crash and one of the enlisted men.
Kneeling, left to right: Winnie Johnson, pilot; Ray Parks, co-pilot; Walt Vukelic, navigator; George Kinder, bombardier, not involved in crash.
Standing, left to right: Robert Schnug, engineer; Robert Woodbeck, radio operator, not involved; Earle Gilman, ball turret gunner, not involved; Elmer Anderson, waist gunner, not involved; Bill Beebe, tail gunner, not involved;

Below: The Squadron's aircraft over enemy occupied territory

Above: *A series of official USAAF photographs taken at the time. Note the complete destruction of the fuselage section, and yet all four men survived.*

beck and Schnug along with 2/Lt Parks barely managed to scramble clear of the shattered wreck before the leaking fuel ignited. In the failing light they were able to locate the other two, but quickly saw that they had suffered serious injuries to their backs. Away from the now blazing bomber two dinghies were inflated and turned over to act as couches for the injured men.

The light drizzle that they had recently been flying through still persisted and mist clung around them. That was the situation when co-pilot, Ray Parks began to walk off to get help. He followed the trail of wreckage back

down the moor and was relieved when he saw the light of a house in the distance.

It was around nine o'clock in the evening when Mrs Tasker answered a knock at the door. A mud and blood bespattered figure stood there.

"We've had a crash," he managed to gasp out. A puzzled Mrs Tasker asked him where he had left his car. Ray Parks had knocked on the door of the Waterman's cottage at Brow Grange, on the edge of the moor. Mr Tasker's father set off to raise the alarm, and a call was put through to the NFS station at Meltham. Within minutes a crew of firemen were

Above: *Officers of the crew, Johnson, Vukelic, Parks and George Kinder who was not on board when the aircraft crashed at Meltham.*

on the scene and they at once set off up the moor as further help was being organised over the 'phone.

By the time that two stretcher parties had arrived at the Waterman's cottage, the firemen had brought Schnug and Woodbeck off the moor, leaving one man with the seriously injured pilot and navigator awaiting stretchers. As the two stretcher parties set off from the cottage they were informed that the fireman, with the two injured crewmen, had a flare pistol from the bomber and would be sending up flares.

After an hour of stumbling around in worsening weather conditions, crossing and re-crossing ravines and bogs, the rescuers found themselves back where they started at the moor's edge. The doctor with the party could carry on no longer and had to be helped back to the cottage. They had expected to see a flare that would have put them in the right direction, but there was nothing to break the darkness that was descending on the moorland.

Leaving two seriously injured men out on the moor all night was out of the question. There was nothing for it but to try again, this time Mr Tasker, with the help of his dog, led the weary rescuers off into the darkness. A further one and a half hours of scrambling around amongst the heather and suddenly one

709th Bomb. Squadron Combat Crews on Review, Rattlesden, Suffolk, England, May, 1945

Above: *Large sections of wreckage partially buried on Meltham Moor.*

of the party stumbled over a propellor which had been shed lower down the moor. They began to shout and at last that long awaited flare shot into the sky, lighting up shards of twisted metal leading in a long trail to where two engines were still burning.

After first aid treatment Johnson and Vukelic were gently lifted onto the stretchers and secured for the trip back to safety. Johnson was conscious and he informed his rescuers that there were five in the crew, that they were from Stowmarket and that the altimeter must have been set wrongly.

At that time there followed some disagreement between the two stretcher parties as to which was the better way to take off the moor. Consequently the party split into two factions and each made its way separately to safety.

The day after the crash an American officer appeared on the scene and instigated a search for the then secret Norden bomb sight, it was a piece of equipment still on the classified list. Upon finding it he immediately left taking the apparatus with him. Following him was a team of American Air Force personnel who proceeded to break up the more substantial pieces of airframe, such as the tail unit, and burying it along with the rest of the wreckage.

This was not accomplished before local youngsters had avoided the policeman on guard and managed to 'win' various interesting items, such as the radio, a gun sight and a flak helmet.

Both Winston Johnson and Walter Vukelic had broken their backs and were confined to wheelchairs. 'Winnie' Johnson died in 1961 as a result of complications arising from the injuries caused in the accident.

Above: *Dick Kinder at the Heritage Centre, Glossop, where an exhibition on aircraft wrecks in the Peak District was staged, in 1988.*

***Sabres XD707 and XD730, 66 Squadron RAF taking part in
Exercise Dividend from Linton on Ouse, crashed Ashop Moor,
22nd July, 1954.***

Map reference 075902 • Map key number 16

As the Second World War ended a new threatening situation began to develop between the Communist bloc and the western nations. It appeared to the military authorities on either side that a third world war seemed ever likely to break out in Europe. As a consequence RAF squadrons that had been disbanded were reformed to add muscle to North Atlantic Treaty Organisation forces. By the '50s Britain had increased her fighter arm to 24 regular squadrons and 20 auxiliary squadrons, equipped with either Meteors or Vampires.

With the sudden outbreak of hostilities between North and South Korea in 1950 and the surprise appearance of the Russian built MIG 15, with its swept back wings, the RAF front line fighters were outdated and outmatched. Defence planners in this country had to consider the possibility of Russian bombers flying on missions against targets in this country, that could outpace our current fighters.

Swept back wing fighters were being developed by Vickers, Hawker and Supermarine but it would be the late '50s before they became available to the RAF. Following close on the heels of the Russians with their wing design were the Americans. Both sides had learned from the German operational jet fighter, the Messerschmitt 262. It was the North American Sabre F86 which was to fill the gap between the slower, straight wing RAF jet fighters and the Hunters and Swifts that were coming off the drawing boards.

In May 1953 the first Sabres were delivered to RAF squadrons in Europe; should hostilities break out the pilots had a worthy match for the Migs. By the end of the year two UK based RAF squadrons were equipped with Canadian built Sabres .

Above: **Alan Green,** at Fassberg in Germany when he was serving with 26 Squadron, flying Vampires.

The distinction of being the very first squadron in this country to be equipped with the new, near supersonic fighter, fell to 66 Squadron based at Linton-on-Ouse. Of the two other squadrons forming the Linton-on-Ouse Wing (92 and 264) 92 Squadron was also chosen to be equipped with the Sabre.

For the pilots in the fighter squadrons the '50s were an exciting period; the days were not too far removed from the Spitfire, Mustang versus Messerschmitt, Focke-Wulfe air fights. A number of pilots in 66 Squadron had battle experience and the younger intake of men were keen to prove their worth among their peers.

Joining 66 Squadron on July 19th, 1954, was an experienced Sabre pilot, Flight Lieutenant Alan Green. Alan was 31 years old and had just missed taking part in the air action against Germany. He had joined the RAF in July, 1943 and was posted to Canada and the flying schools operating there. After training to fly single-engined aircraft he was returned to England in December, 1944 to complete his fighter pilots' course. He could only watch as the weeks slipped by and the defeat of Germany drew speedily to its close. He finished his training as the war in the Far East ended.

The armed forces of the nations were being wound-down in 1946 and he was released in May of that year. Returning to civilian life as an engineer near Walsall, Alan found it difficult to settle and applied to re-enlist. He was dismayed to find that the RAF were only prepared to offer him the rank of Flight Sergeant. He refused to take a demotion and wrote to the then Prime Minister, Clement Attlee. His letter was passed on to the Air Chief Marshall, Sir Leslie Hollinghurst, who promptly arranged a meeting and sorted the matter out. Flight Lieutenant Alan Green found himself at the famous fighter station at Biggin Hill, and at the start of a new career flying his nation's first jet fighters, the Meteor and Vampire. He was posted to Fassberg in Germany and 98 Squadron. Later he was transferred to 26 Squadron where he served as a flight commander. At the time that he joined them they were flying the Vampire twin-boomed fighter, but then in November, 1953 the pilots were thrilled to receive the Sabre.

It was a new era — along with the swept-wing fighter went new flying garb for the pilot; an anti-G suit and a hard helmet, or bone dome, to fit over the regular flying helmet. They felt that they had taken a leap ahead technically and applied themselves to practising air combat at much increased speeds.

The Sabre cockpit was roomier and the instrument panel looked daunting, with more dials and clocks than the British jets of the day. Control was power assisted, unlike the Meteor and Vampire which required physical effort to operate the rudder and control column; a touch of the controls and the hydraulic assistance caused the Sabre to respond immediately. Whilst it was an easy aircraft to fly, there were a number of accidents among the fighter squadrons operating on the continent, mainly due to inexperience and problems with the hydraulics.

Because of Alan Green's experience and skill as a flyer (he was rated as above average on both navigating and instrument flying) he received a posting to the Central Flying School at South Cerney, where he was to train as an instructor. The Provost jet trainer seemed so tame after the Sabre and he soon missed the exciting atmosphere of a front line squadron. There was the problem, for him, of constantly telling others what to do — he found that unpleasant. He could do no other than request a return to squadron duties. The usual procedure in those days, should any trainee instructor renege, was to blacklist him, however, in the case of Alan Green it had been observed by the instructors that he had conducted himself conscientiously throughout the course. The CO was pleased to permit him to select the squadron of his choice and return to operational flying. He chose a posting to 66 Squadron, one of the only two Sabre squadrons operating in this country.

When Alan Green arrived at Linton in July, 1954, the annual air defence exercise, which on that occasion had been given the code name Operation Dividend, was underway. It was the largest exercise that had ever been carried out by the RAF since the end of the Second World War. In order to test the defences of this country 'enemy' aircraft, represented by Continental based RAF Canberra bombers and American B-47s, would fly sorties over Britain. The defending fighters had the job of intercepting them and chasing them off. All good fun, especially so on the occasions when Canadian built Sabres appeared in the skies over this country along with the attacking bombers, then a Sabre versus Sabre melee would take place. The gun cameras would click away recording possible 'hits' and a good time was had by all.

Because he was a new arrival at the Squadron in July, 1954, Alan Green was excluded from the Command exercise. He had to be given time to familiarise himself with the local terrain. Indeed, he carried out his first familiarisation

Below: *Alan Green in the cockpit of a Sabre, whilst he was serving in Germany with 26 Squadron.*

Above: *Re-oxygenating a Sabre during a 'turn round' at Linton-on-Ouse.*

flight on July 19th. He went on to fly a practise interception two days later, July 21st. The following day one of the pilots taking part in the exercise went sick and at once Alan Green volunteered to take his place in a section of four aircraft. One of his former colleagues said at the time, "Alan did not hesitate, he was as keen as mustard."

He would be taking up position number two in the second pair of Sabres, and would be flying as wingman to a pilot ten years his junior. At that time Alan Green had flown 55 hours on the Sabre Mark 4 and consequently was one of the experienced pilots in 66 Squadron on the type. He had flown the Sabre to its limits; shortly after transferring from Vampires to Sabres he had joined the ever growing band of Sabre pilots to go through the much-talked-about sound barrier, by diving the aircraft vertically from 40,000 feet.

It didn't particularly bother Alan that he wasn't to fly in the lead position — after all he was the new boy of the Squadron. He was just pleased to be taking part in the exercise. The formation consisted of: Leader first pair, Sergeant Bruce McDonald, wingman Sergeant Charlie Spinks; Leader second pair, Flying Officer Jim Horne and his wingman Flight Lieutenant Alan Green.

On Thursday, July 22nd, at 6.25pm the four Sabres took off for the third and last time that day. Radar had once more picked up 'enemy' intruders and they were to intercept and chase them off, for as long as their fuel permitted. Alan was at the controls of XD730 and his leader, Flying Officer James Horne, who was 21 years old, was flying XD707.

It took the four fighters twenty minutes to reach 38,000 feet where they could expect to find 'bandits'. After a futile visual search of the skies, the

Above: *A pair of Sabres taking off during 'Exercise Dividend'.*

section leader, Sergeant McDonald, called over the radio that they would return to base. The four Sabres came around and began a descent towards the vast carpet of cloud stretching out beneath them. The time was around seven o'clock as they reached 12,000 feet and entered the clouds.

Visual contact between the four aircraft vanished in the swirling wetness. Horne's radio was acting up and he reported that he was only receiving weak signals. Enwrapped in the cloud blanket, McDonald was watching his altimetre and at 5,000 feet he called out to the others not to drop below 3,800. They were on a direct line for Linton — minutes from home, at the speed they were travelling.

It was after seven o'clock when the Kinder Reservoir keeper, Mr Vernon Bennett, heard a noise like thunder. Cloud shrouded the hills and it was raining heavily as he turned to look in the direction of the noise. Two jet aircraft were thundering up the valley, having just dropped through a hole in the overcast. He had never seen the like

of it before — planes had never come so low down in that area. They presented a thrilling spectacle as they roared along at 1,000 feet plus above the valley bottom. Vernon Bennett remembered thinking to himself that the planes would have to climb sharply if they were to clear the 2,000 foot high mountain top directly in their flight path. As quickly as they had appeared they were swallowed up in clouds which sat atop Kinder.

The official account states that the two Sabres flew into the ground killing both pilots instantly. However, two climbers were later to claim that they met a rambler who told them that he had just seen the aircraft collide. The two men, who were members of the Royal Observer Corps and so knew the type, said that the Sabres passed below them before climbing to get over Kinder. The man whom they met on the path told them that when the collision occurred there was a terrible clatter, 'it was as if a hundred dustbins had been banged together'. He went on to describe how the 'planes had touched and bits flew off them as one went into a flat spin and the other began to roll. The whole scenario had been quickly swallowed up in cloud.

Back at Linton the leader of the section, Sergeant McDonald and his wingman landed, they were unable to explain the disappearance of the other two. Attempts to raise them on the radio had been futile and when flying time ran out for pilots Green and Horne, distress procedure was instigated.

The reservoir keeper was unaware that an accident had occurred and so was unable to alert the authorities. For some reason the two climbers failed to report what they had been told until some time after the event. The rambler, who claimed that he saw what happened and told the climbers, has never been identified. Because the Pennine hills were completely covered in cloud for the next two days, the tragedy was hidden from searching aircraft. For some of the men in 66 Squadron it was like re-running an old film — two of their fighters had gone missing three years earlier, and had later been found scattered on the hills (see the story on page 53). It was to be the same again.

It was 2.15pm on Sunday afternoon,

Below: *With the Sabre fighter aircraft technology took a mighty step forward; here the Squadron Commander at Linton-on-Ouse, Squadron Leader Dennis Usher, is seen climbing into his mount in the fighting gear of the '50s.*

three days later when a walker, Graham Atkin, coming across the moor from Hayfield heading for the Snake road, came across wreckage. He first saw a body wearing a flying suit, then pieces of metal scattered for as far as he could see. He reported his grim find to the authorities and soon search and recover parties were being formed in Hayfield, Glossop and Edale. Joining the ramblers and Peak Park wardens were elements of the RAF Mountain Rescue Team from Harpur Hill, Buxton. Recovery of the bodies was made difficult because of the wet and boggy nature of the terrain, but eventually the remains were taken to Whaley Bridge mortuary.

At an inquest the following Tuesday the Coroner stated that he could see no apparent reason why the aircraft were flying so low. Time of the crash was established by the broken watch on Horne's wrist which indicated that impact had occurred at nine minutes past seven.

What had led the pilots to drop so low in the area? Perhaps the hole in the overcast held the answer; they must have seen the hole and like all daytime pilots, they would have been happier to drop through it and out of the 'pea soup' where they could see the ground and then establish their position. Did they collide once they had climbed back into the cloud? Judging from the point of impact it would seem likely.

The coroner in his summing up stated that: "For some reason, which at the moment is not explained, it appears that the two aircraft were too low. Whereas they normally flew at 40 to 50,000 feet, they were flying at only 1,200 to 1,500 feet and crashed into the side of Kinder Scout. But there is always the question of human error. Verdict, misadventure!"

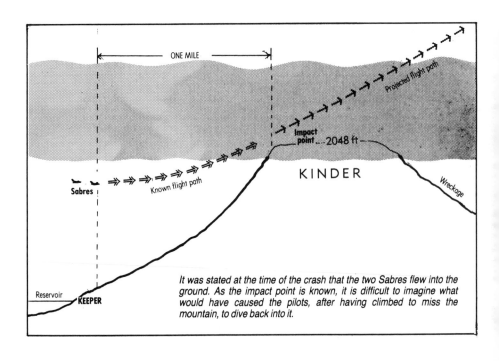

It was stated at the time of the crash that the two Sabres flew into the ground. As the impact point is known, it is difficult to imagine what would have caused the pilots, after having climbed to miss the mountain, to dive back into it.

Above: **Flying Officer James Horne**

Above: *A section of the wing from Horne's aircraft, still with the number '707' showing faintly.*

Above: *Parts of one of the engines scattered across the boggy ground; some of the metal impervious to rust.*
Below: *A tail unit section.*

Above: *A tail fin from one of the two fighters; it is no longer possible to identify which one.*

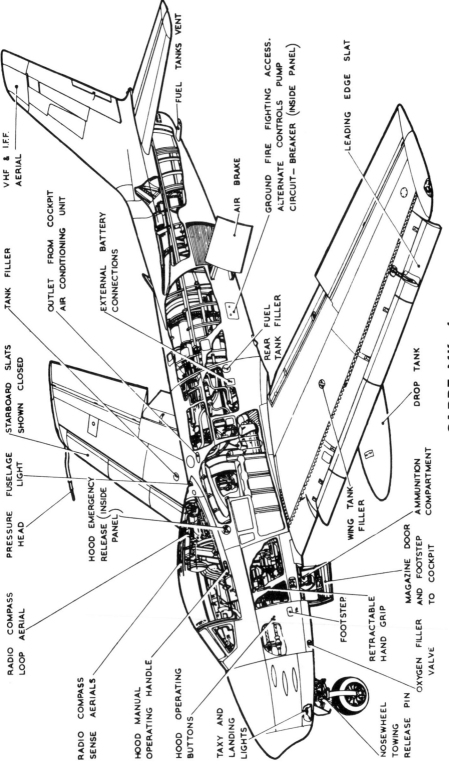

RADIO COMPASS LOOP AERIAL

PRESSURE HEAD

FUSELAGE LIGHT

STARBOARD SLATS SHOWN CLOSED

TANK FILLER

OUTLET FROM COCKPIT AIR CONDITIONING UNIT

EXTERNAL BATTERY CONNECTIONS

VHF & I.F.F. AERIAL

FUEL TANKS VENT

AIR BRAKE

GROUND FIRE FIGHTING ACCESS. ALTERNATE CONTROLS PUMP CIRCUIT—BREAKER (INSIDE PANEL)

LEADING EDGE SLAT

REAR FUEL TANK FILLER

DROP TANK

WING TANK FILLER

AMMUNITON COMPARTMENT

RADIO COMPASS SENSE AERIALS

HOOD MANUAL OPERATING HANDLE

HOOD OPERATING BUTTONS

TAXY AND LANDING LIGHTS

HOOD EMERGENCY RELEASE (INSIDE PANEL)

MAGAZINE DOOR AND FOOTSTEP TO COCKPIT

FOOTSTEP

RETRACTABLE HAND GRIP

OXYGEN FILLER VALVE

NOSEWHEEL TOWING RELEASE PIN

SABRE MK. 4

Anson NL185, Halton HQ Flight RAF Bomber Command, on a flight from Halton to Feltwell, crashed The Cloughs, November 23rd, 1945.

Map reference 089866 ● Map key number 17

The Dark Peak District of Derbyshire has, over the years, brought an abrupt end to the flying careers of many promising, and skilled, airmen. This was probably the result, in some cases, of treating the high ground without due respect; or treating local 'hops' in a relaxed manner. The untimely end of one skilled pilot demonstrated the folly of failing to take into consideration England's highest mountain range.

Wing Commander Richard Douglas Speare, DSO, DFC and Bar, Croix de Guerre with Palme, was killed after apparently setting a wrong course on his compass, and flying into the hills.

Those who knew him, and had flown with him during the war that had just ended, were puzzled as to how a pilot of his standard and experience could have made such a mistake by flying on a wrong bearing. He was considered to be one of the most experienced pilots in Bomber Command.

For eleven months of the war, from June 1943 to May 1944, 'Dickie' Speare had been the Commanding Officer of one of the RAF's secret squadrons, Number 138 Squadron. That special unit, along with 161 Squadron had been engaged in clandestine operations over enemy occupied territory. 161 Squadron shared a base at Tempsford, and was mainly responsible for flying agents in and out of France using Westland Lysanders. Whereas, 138 Squadron began to specialise in long distance flights to Poland and Czechoslovakia dropping agents, weapons and supplies. That type of operation required maximum ability from pilots and navigators. It meant that the crews had to fly at night to a field a thousand miles away, locating it by a pin-prick of light on the ground. Once the drop had taken place the return trip had to be made, avoiding heavily defended areas and nightfighters — it all required airmanship of the highest order.

Being the Commanding Officer of 138 Squadron, Dickie Speare was not required to fly on every sortie, but he certainly flew as pilot on some of the missions. The late Wing Commander J. C. Corby remembered flying with him on an operation to Norway on October 15th,

1943. The trip was made in a Halifax II and the code name for the operation was 'Goldfinch 1'. It was an uneventful trip, the drop zone was clearly marked and the supply of arms and ammunition was dropped by parachute to the waiting partisans. They landed back at Kinloss in Scotland, returning to Tempsford the following day.

Although as a general rule squadron commanding officers were not called upon to do as many 'ops' as the regular crews, Dickie Speare was flying on operations at least once a month during his time with 138 Squadron. When the 'Wingco' decided to fly one of the missions himself, then a volunteer crew was brought together. One such crew member was Colin Mather; his regular crew had just finished their tour of ops and that left him a spare 'bod', so he volunteered to fly with the Wingco. He flew with him to Southern France on the night of February 7th, 1944. Again on March 6th to another location in France — the flight duration on that trip was seven hours.

They were nerve racking times, for to avoid the enemy radar it meant heading for the enemy coast at wave-top height, then shortly before landfall climbing to 7,000 feet in order to avoid the light flak defences. Once over the heavily defended coastal area, the pilot would nose down the Halifax to tree top height and race for the drop zone.

Operations over Holland took a nasty turn when the German sercret service (Abwehr) succeeded in infiltrating the Dutch Underground. As a result of that penetration, captured wireless operators were made to transmit false messages through to Special Operations Executive HQ. Despite the operators leaving out previously arranged code words, which were deliberately put in for such a contingency, the receivers in Britain could not believe that every wireless operator in Holland had been captured.

They chose to ignore their own briefing instructions to foreign based operators and accepted as genuine the radio messages. The ones to suffer were 161 and 138 Squadrons as they continued to drop agents and supplies at the enemy's direction — then fly the gauntlet of the alerted fighters. Losses were heavy as Dickie Speare took over command of 138 Squadron.

To make matters worse, the Germans were improving their air defences in answer to the British and American bomber offensive against German cities. More and more Halifax II's of 138 Squadron were marked up 'FTR' (failed to return). That reached a climax in September 1943 when seven aircraft failed to return out of sixteen that had set out for secret destinations in occupied Poland. Out of those that did return most of them were so badly damaged by flak that they were being repaired for many weeks. The situation was eased somewhat with the arrival of three Liberator bombers, with their long range capability. They came just in time to help out the only two servicable Halifax left in 138 Squadron. With the increased range potential of the new American Liberators, it meant that the planners at 138 could route the aircraft away from heavily defended areas. That was achieved by flying them to Poland by way of, and over, neutral Sweden. Flight duration for that trip worked out at around thirteen hours — a long time for crews to concentrate and navigate by dead reckoning and map reading. A radio guidance system was introduced in the winter of 1943, but some time was to pass before it could be used to its best advantage.

It was while he was serving with 138 Squadron that he received the Bar to his Distinguished Flying Cross. Further, for his work with the secret squadron, he was awarded the Distinguished Service Order in July 1944. By that time he had

Above: *Fifth from the left is Dickie Speare, seen here at Driffield, Yorkshire, when he served with 75 Squadron. In the background are Harrow Mk1 bombers, thus helping to date the photograph as being taken in the late '30s.*

received a posting to the RAF Bomber Development Unit at Newmarket.

Sir Lewis Hodges, who had been responsible for tactical developments at Bomber Command, recalled Dickie Speare during that particular period.

"I visited the Bomber Development Unit both officially to see Dickie Speare and to go to the races. Dickie was instrumental in arranging for me to fly the Mosquito — which I hadn't done before — also the Halifax Mk III. Dickie and I were working together on a new device called AGLT (Automatic Gun Laying Turret). It was a radar controlled gun turret that never did work very well. I was doing one or two flights at the BDU and Dickie was flying the Lancaster with the new turret. I remember him as an outstanding pilot — that was presumably why he was sent to the Bomber Development Unit in the first place. He was a most congenial companion, a very human, sympathetic and considerate officer, who was very

well liked and respected by everyone. It came as a great shock to me when I heard that he had been killed flying — of all things — an Anson, after all he had been through operationally."

Dickie Speare had reached the pinnacle of his distinguished RAF career when he died so tragically. His career in the RAF had begun back in 1936 when he had been granted a Short Service Commission as an Acting Pilot Officer in the General Duties Branch of the RAF — he was twenty years old. After training he was posted for five months to 38 Squadron, based at Mildenhall. It was a night bomber unit flying the fixed undercarriage Fairey Hendons. It was whilst he was on a course with 206 Squadron for a month that he first flew the Avro Anson, the aircraft type in which he would later lose his life. He went on to spend three years with 75 Squadron, which operated the Harrow bomber, then later the Wellington — the change to a modern bomber with a retractable undercarriage came just in time for the outbreak of the Second World War. In March 1939, 75 Squadron had become, what was later to be known as, an Operational Training Unit.

Dickie Speare received promotion to Flight Lieutenant and was posted to 15 Operational Training Unit where he helped to train bomber crews. He was Officer Commanding 'A' Flight with the rank of Acting Squadron Leader and spent many hours flying as First Pilot on Wellingtons, training pilots and helping to process crews for Bomber Command. He saw many crews leave the OTU to join front line squadrons and yet he himself had never flown a single operation over Germany. His request for a transfer to an operational squadron was eventually successful and he received a posting to 7 Squadron, based at Oakington.

The very first squadron in the RAF to be equipped with four-engined bombers was 7 Squadron and they had been operating the Stirling for nine months when Dickie Speare joined. A week after arriving at Oakington he was assigned to fly on his first mission. The target for the night of May 23rd, 1941 was the German city of Cologne and in order to give him some first hand experience he was assigned to the crew of Flying Officer Blacklock, DFM, as Second Pilot. They took off from Oakington with six other Stirlings and headed for the enemy coast.

Once over the target the bomb-aimer, Sergeant Ashton, took his position in the nose of the Stirling and the aircraft's bomb doors were opened. However, Ashton discovered that he was unable to release the bombs — an electrical fault. There was nothing for it but to turn for home. As they approached Holland on the way back the fault was put right — it was a bad electrical earth. Rather than bring the bombs back the 'Skipper' decided to dump the load on the port of Rotterdam. The Squadron had attacked the oil storage tanks there three months earlier, on their very first bombing raid of the war. The five one thousand pounders and the fourteen five hundred pounders were successfully dropped and were seen to explode on the docks far below.

The following day Squadron Leader Dickie Speare was appointed Officer Commanding 'A' Flight and was assigned a regular crew: Sergeant G. C. Bayley (Second Pilot); Pilot Officer E. D. Levien (Navigator); Sergeant E. C. Glenwright (Wireless Operator); Sergeant R. W. Peters (Bomb Aimer/Front Gunner); Sergeant A. J. Graham (Rear Gunner) and Sergeant D. H. Williams (Flight Engineer).

The first sortie of the new crew took place the next night when they were briefed to search out and bomb the German heavy cruiser 'Hipper'. Seven Stirlings of 7 Squadron set out on the mission, but the 'Hipper' wasn't in the place it was supposed to be and after a fruitless search the aircraft returned with their bomb loads.

Throughout the month of June, 1941, targets followed in quick succession: Huls, Dusseldorf, Brest, Kiel, Bremen and Hamburg. On the trip to Kiel an enemy nightfighter located Dickie Speare's Stirling and, before he could shake it off with some fancy flying, they sustained some damage to the starboard wing. The fuel tanks in the wings were missed, but numerous holes were punched through the flap. Cannon shells slammed into the fuselage cutting through some hydraulic pipes. The loss of fluid from these rendered the rear gun turret unserviceable. They landed back at base safely.

On the trip to Hamburg they sustained some damage which made their landing back at base 'hairy'. As they approached the target Dickie Speare had opened the bomb doors and they were

Above: *Wing Commander Dickie Speare*

flying straight and level. It was always a tense time for the crew, once the bombs were gone the Skipper would be able to take evasive action, but until then the bomb aimer needed a steady platform. They felt so vulnerable with the bomb doors open and all those high explosives suspended in the bomb bays. What they hadn't realised was, that they had already sustained some flak damage to the underside of the aircraft and shrapnel had cut into one of the bomb doors. Shortly after having heard the call over the intercom, 'bombs away!' Dickie Speare banked sharply from the target area and took a bearing for base. The usual check was made to make sure that the bomb bays were empty — then what all crews dreaded came over the intercom "We've got a hang-up Skipper!"

One 500 pound bomb had failed to drop — its release mechanism had been damaged. No amount of coaxing would persaude it to part company from them, they were faced with the prospect of landing with it.

Over the Oakington circuit Dickie Speare informed the control tower that they were coming in to land with a serious problem on board. Gently as he could he lined up the runway and settled the bomber down. The landing was gentle enough but that didn't prevent the 500 pounder from jolting free and smacking onto the concrete runway — however, it failed to explode.

The crew made just three trips in July and on one of them a Dutch passenger was aboard, for what purpose it was not stated. The target city was Munster, but bad weather over the target made it impossible to carry out the attack. On the return trip Dickie Speare considered dropping the bomb load on Rotterdam, as was the usual practise, but thought better of it in view of his passenger.

On their fifth mission in the month of August the target was Duisburg and they came near to being brought down. A burst of flak close to the nose of the Stirling blew away most of the cockpit cover seriously injuring the Second Pilot, Sergeant Bayley. Also the rear gunner, Sergeant Graham was wounded by another accurate flak burst. It was an uncomfortable return trip with the slipstream whipping over the flight deck and through the fuselage. Dickie Speare managed to fly the bomber back under the most difficult conditions.

In September Dickie Speare made his first trip to the big 'B' (Berlin). Bombs were seen to burst on the target area. Incendiaries started large fires and it was an enthusiastic Squadron Leader who landed back at Oakington to report a 'wizard prang'.

For his skill in bringing back the Stirling with the shattered cockpit canopy he was mentioned in despatches on September 24th, 1941. During the following month he was awarded the Distinguished Flying Cross having completed 25 operations against the enemy with 7 Squadron.

As a 'blooded' and experienced pilot he received a posting to 1651 Heavy Conversion Unit as Commanding Officer, where he spent most of 1942. The purpose of the unit was to take bomber crews to the final stage before being posted to an operational bomber squadron. Crews were converting from twin-engined aircraft, Wellingtons, to four-engined Stirlings and taking on another crew member — a flight engineer. He completed the year with the Bomber Development Unit at RAF Gransden Lodge, Manchester, where technical development and new equipment were tried out. The unit operated with Lancasters.

He returned to operations in January, 1943, with a posting to an Australian squadron, 460 Squadron, RAAF. As he had been off operations for almost eighteen months, he did his first sortie with the Commanding Officer, Wing Commander C. E. Martin. The target was Berlin and in Lancaster ED369 Dickie Speare was on the flight deck as Second Pilot. On the outward journey the port inner engine failed and the bombs were jettisoned in the region of Hamburg.

Two days later with an all Australian regular crew he took off for Essen along with eleven other aircraft from the Squadron. He flew with that crew throughout his time with 460 Squadron, flying fourteen missions in all. His reputation was such, that in June 1943, he was posted to the Squadron where his skills would be tested to the utmost — the 'cloak and dagger' unit, 138 Squadron. He was to spend eleven vital months with 138 and received a Bar to his DFC, then in July 1944 he received

the Distinguished Service Order. The citation read:
"Since being awarded a Bar to his DFC this officer has completed many sorties which have demanded a high degree of skill and resolution. He has at all times displayed great keenness and determination and his gallant example has inspired all with whom he has flown."

Before the war ended the French awarded him the Croix-de-Guerre with Palme. His last assignment of the war was to go on the Special Duties List for the United States of America, and he sailed for there in July 1945. He was bound for the Army Corp Staff College with the rank of Wing Commander.

After four months in the States, Dickie Speare was back in England and at Bomber Command HQ, RAF Halton with the Communication Flight.

On Friday morning, November 23rd, at 10.50am Wing Commander Dickie Speare climbed into Anson NL185 to ferry it to Feltwell. His personal trunks and cases were stashed in the narrow fuselage between the six seats. All radio equipment had been removed from NL185 and the visibility along the flight path between Buckinghamshire and Norfolk was poor. He had submitted a flight plan to Air Traffic Control which would take the Anson to the east coast of Lincolnshire.

At Feltwell, Wing Commander Speare was reported overdue.

A twenty years old farmer's son, Edward Gordon Cooper of Highfield Head Farm was rounding up his father's cattle on Edale Moors. As he approached the 'Woolpacks', a high crop of rocks, he looked down on a scene of devastation. The wreckage of the Anson was scattered across the hillside. Beside the shattered cockpit lay the body of the pilot — above his left breast pocket were a row of medal ribbons, awards from the recently finished war. All around were suitcases with their contents spilled out.

The RAF Mountain Rescue Service, based at Harpur Hill, Buxton, attended to the crash. The body was carried by the stretcher party over marsh bog and moorland stream, down a steep hillside to an ambulance that had been brought up the rough track, which led from the village of Edale to the footbridge at the bottom of what is known as 'Jacob's Ladder'. The remains were taken from there to the RAF Station mortuary at Buxton. He left a wife and son; their home was at Scholes Park Road, Scarborough.

The scene of the accident was far removed from the course that he should have been on. It was suggested that Dickie Speare had inadvertently set his compass incorrectly. From Halton to Feltwell it was necessary to fly on a bearing of 030 degrees and yet his actual course was 330 degrees. The question remained: how could a pilot of Wing Commander Dickie Speare's standard and experience have made such an incredible mistake? Could it have been

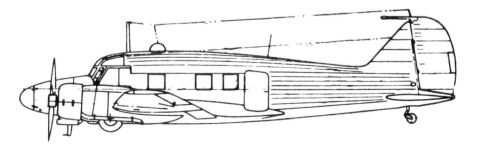

the case that he was relaxed and overconfident, looking forward to a good long holiday and treated familiar things in a cursory way?

Sir Lewis Hodges, who knew Dickie Speare well, always had great difficulty in accepting the account of the wrong compass setting:

"I heard about the death of Dickie Speare when I was in Palestine, and although I was told about the compass story — I found it hard to believe, as it was most unlikely that there would be as gross an error as that in any compass. I remember at the time thinking that it would be almost impossible for a pilot as experienced as he, to finish up in the Pennines."

Below: *One of the Cheetah engines remains at the site and used to carry a simple typed memorial to Dickie Speare.*

Miles Hawk G-AJSF Blackpool and Fylde Aero Club, on a flight from Squires Gate to Barton, crashed Kinder Low End, July 29th, 1957.

Map reference 074868 ● Map key number 18

It was a Sunday afternoon and Mr and Mrs Arthur Jones of Audenshaw were out on the moors for a day's walking. They were on Kinder Scout and at around 1.55 they had stopped for a bite to eat. As they sat there they heard an aero engine and they spotted, coming towards them just beneath the clouds, a single engine aeroplane.

The pilot must have seen the high ground in front of him, for he banked away towards Kinder Low. The aircraft disappeared from their sight behind some intervening ground and there followed a loud bang — then silence.

They hurried to the area where they thought the sound came from, but it was half an hour before they came upon what was obviously a fuel tank. Not too far away they stumbled across the crumpled form of the pilot. A quick examination and they realised that they could do nothing for him, his neck appeared to be broken. The aircraft wreckage lay close by, scattered across the moorland.

A group of hikers arrived at the spot and Arthur Jones decided to go and raise the alarm. Leaving his wife at the site he began to trot the two miles down the hillside to Tunstead House where he telephoned the police. When they arrived he guided them back up the Kinder to the crash site. Fire engines and an ambulance were only able to get to Coldwell Clough Farm.

The pilot, William Warburton Hall, aged 35 of St Annes had been flying from Squires Gate, Blackpool to Barton, Manchester to visit relatives. He was 20 miles beyond his destination, pushed along by a 30 knot tail wind. He had not obtained a weather report when he had taken off and so was unaware of the strong westerly wind.

Hall had taken off at 1.30 pm, for what should have been a 15 minute flight, and ended up on Kinder at 1.55.

An engineer at Squires Gate Airport, who was also a Blackpool and Fylde Aero Club member said, "When Mr Hall left, although there was a fair amount of cloud about, it was sunny and conditions were not really adverse for flying."

William Hall was regarded as a very good pilot and had served in the RAF during the war — he left a wife and two children.

Experts trying to determine the reason for the crash were hindered by the theft of numerous instruments from the wrecked cockpit. The Coroner, Mr F. R. Nesbitt, appealed to the public not to pilfer articles from crashed aircraft, as it prevented the investigators from discovering the reason for the crash and thus help avoid future accidents.

By the late fifties dozens of aircraft had come to grief on the Pennines and walkers were helping themselves to bits and pieces to take away as souvenirs. In some cases belts of live ammunition was being located and dug up. Scavenging from the sites is still going on.

Harvard FT415 Flying Training School, on a training flight from Syreston, crashed Wool Packs, January 14th, 1952.

Map reference 088868 • Map key number 19

It was a Saturday afternoon and four hikers from Manchester had arrived at Edale by train. The intention was to walk back across the Pennines heading for Hayfield. The hills were covered in deep snow and it was hard going up the steep path known as Jacobs Ladder. As they neared the top of their climb one of them saw a strange object in the near distance — yellow metal stood out against the white of the snow.

They made their way across the intervening ground and were shocked at what they found. It was a training aircraft that had hit the hill, wrecking it completely. Both wings had been ripped away; the engine and front of the aeroplane were buried in the ground; the fuselage and tail were still recognisable. Around the cockpit area there had been an intense fire — seated in the cockpit was the body of the pilot.

The hikers hurried back down the hillside to raise the alarm at Tunstead Guest House, where Mr S. F. Forrester alerted the police and the RAF Mountain Rescue Team at Harpur Hill, Buxton.

It was dark when the police and RAF personnel climbed the mountain to try and find the crash site. With the aid of torches a party of three eventually found the aeroplane and alerted the other search parties — it was 8.20 pm. By 10 o'clock the body had been removed from the cockpit and fastened to a sledge. The sledge was dragged over deep snow drifts to Bamford and the men left the site after many hours on the snow covered moorland.

Above: *A section of fuselage that was taken away by the maintenance team attending the crash.*

Constable Starkey from New Mills had been among the three who had found the Harvard trainer. After more than six hours trudging through deep snow and standing about in the bitter cold he was at last back at New Mills police station. He had rested, had hot drinks and something to eat when two RAF police drove up to the station. There was no way of identifying the pilot from the remains they brought off the moor — they needed to return at once to the site and required a guide. It was four o'clock on Sunday morning when Constable Starkey, along with another officer, set off for the crashed plane.

The pilot was 20 years old, Fleet Air Arm Midshipman Brian Farley of Briarfield Road, Heaton Chapel, Stockport. He had been missing for six days whilst on a routine training flight from Syerston, Nottinghamshire to Kemble in Cirencester, Gloucestershire. The reason why he had not been discovered sooner was the fact that he was 60 miles off course — it had not been thought necessary to look for him so far north.

On the course that he was on, Farley would have passed over his home town of Stockport had not the hills got in the way. It has been suggested by some that perhaps he had been engaged in the usual pilot's practice of getting a bird's eye view of his native town. A common enough desire for any pilot, but if that was the case, then the desire led to his death.

Below: *Small fragments are to be found at the site today.*

Hampden AE381, 50 Squadron RAF, returning from operations to Skellingthorpe, crashed Cluther Rocks, January 21st, 1942.

Map reference 078875 • Map key number 20

Living conditions at RAF Swinderby's satellite field were primitive in 1942. Huts seemed to be scattered about at random and placed in such a way as to cause maximum inconvenience to the occupiers. Frost and snow made life miserable for the Hampden crews who had recently moved to Skellingthorpe from Scampton. At that period some of the squadrons were in the throes of re-equipping with Manchester bombers and, the satellite field had been given over to the operation of the obsolescent Handley Page Hampden.

A new crew of four had come together and would fly on operations with 50 Squadron. Two of the sergeants were Australians, the pilot Sergeant J. W. C. (Ginger) Heron and navigator, Sergeant Walter Chantler Williams (who as a lad had emigrated with his mother and brother from South Shields).

The wireless operator was English, Sergeant W. Tromans, and so was the air gunner Sergeant Sidney Albert Peters ('Boy') from West Wickham, Kent.

Sid (Boy) Peters wrote to his brother, who was in the Royal Tank Corps, and complained of the spartan conditions at Skellingthorpe — describing it as 'a hell of a camp'. It was never intended to be staffed with flying crews, rather the idea was for the crews to drive in from Swinderby, seven miles away, to pick up kit and take off. The mess was a 20 minutes walk from the scattered huts tucked away in some trees, that served as sleeping quarters. The ablutions were a 20 minutes walk in the opposite direction; there were no bath huts. One of the reasons the crews had been given for operating from Skellingthorpe was that the runways at Swinderby were unserviceable during certain winter months.

Sid Peters described the Australian personnel as a pretty tough bunch, who were engaged in various covert flying activities. Also he mentioned that his Australian fellow crew members lived life 'fast'. They were beginning to come together as a team and were ready to take their place on operations.

By way of a warming up mission, the new crew were scheduled to fly a leaflet dropping sortie over occupied Europe, on the evening of January 21st, 1942. A letter to his brother, just a few days before the fatal flight, had a depressed air about it:

"Shan't be sorry when all this is done with now. Don't know that I shall mind much if I never fly again when it's all over. The old crowd has got a bit thin now — out of the original 20 of us on the final course there are not more than a dozen of us left."

Presumably these men had been lost on operations.

Prior to their flight the crew had been fully briefed on how they could obtain navigational assistance from beacons, searchlights and 'Darky' (this was a system where aerodromes listened on a common frequency and picked up aircraft transmissions, took bearings, then compared them with other fields by telephone; the resulting information was then relayed to the pilot). The weather was bad over France and Heron must have decided to turn for base without dropping the leaflets.

At Ringway, Manchester, the RAF personnel were alerted that a bomber was returning from a mission and was 50 miles off course and heading for them. They would have to take over and help to guide the bomber in.

Herbert Ward of Royton, Lancashire was on duty in the radio room that night and remembered his colleagues picking up Morse Code signals from the bomber. Using the Direction Finding equipment they began to bring the aircraft in. The crew were flying in from the southwest on the radio beam being transmitted from Ringway. The sound of the engines was heard as the Hampden passed overhead unseen in the blizzard that was blowing up. Heron was contacted and instructed to make a 180 degree turn and come back along the radio beam.

As the men sat there in silence gazing at the crackling radio equipment the telephone rang — it was the police station at Hayfield. They were asking for a search party to be sent as they had received a report that an aircraft had crashed into the mountain. As it was a few hours to dawn, and the stint for the men on duty was nearly over, the Commanding Officer at Ringway, who had been alerted, decided to use some of them to make up the search party.

So it was that Herbert Ward found himself, after a night on duty, standing outside in the snow awaiting a lorry to take him, eleven others and an officer to search for the crashed aircraft. The sky was beginning to lighten as the RAF search team arrived at Hayfield and were directed to the local gamekeeper's cottage.

They found the gamekeeper, John Watson, in a distressed state and he was being comforted by his wife. He had heard the bomber pass overhead and then the sound of the crash. He had tried to reach the crashed bomber, but all his attempts had been frustrated by the deep snow drifts. He had however, got close enough on one occasion to see some of the four-man crew in the burning aircraft. No matter how he tried he could not reach them, the soft, deep, banked up snow proved an effective barrier to the, by then, near exhausted gamekeeper. He had finally stumbled back down the hillside in tears to be comforted and to await a rescue team.

Herbert Ward remembered that night vividly:

"After being served with a hot drink we set out up the mountainside dragging sledges behind us to carry the dead or

Above: **Billy Tromans,** *wireless operator.*
Right: **Ginger Heron,** *pilot (Australian).*
Below: **Albert 'Boy' Peters,** *air gunner.*

Above: *Walter Williams,* navigator (Australian).

injured. It wasn't easy going — our hob-nailed service boots and long, heavy greatcoats were totally unsuited for the purpose. Eventually we reached the top and made our way towards the Hampden that way. The bomber had hit the last few feet of the hilltop — another foot or two and it would have cleared it.

"There was nothing to be done except release the dead crew members from the wreckage and strap them to the sledges. I remember that the pilot had ginger hair and that he was an Australian. It was about 4 pm in the afternoon when we finally reached the bottom again and met the ambulance. The police had laid on a meal for us at the local pub where the locals extended their hospitality to us until about 9 pm when we finally set out for Ringway."

One of the farmers in the area, Harold Hodgson, of Hill House Farm, Hayfield, also remembered the night of the crash and leaflets scattered about over his fields — he regrets not having kept one. Had he done so, we may have known a little more about the destination and reason for that sortie on the night of January 21st, 1942. The records of 50 Squadron contain no mention of the accident, or of a flight on the night of the blizzard. The form 1180 (crash card) held at the Air Historical Branch of the RAF gives the following information:

Date 21/1/42. Hampden I AE 381. Pair Pegasus engines. Time, 20.38. Place, North of Peak Kinder Scout. Fire on impact. Pilot, JWC Heron, Sgt, 404820, Australian. All the crew of four killed. A/C had signalled 'bad visibility' and had then flown into the mountain. The A/C was approximately 50 miles off course. Neither the pilot nor navigator were experienced. The O/C said that the crew had been fully briefed prior to departure on how to obtain navigational assist- ance.

The air gunner, Sid Peters, had only been married three months when the accident happened. His wife Joan, who had joined the Auxilliary Fire Service to do her bit in the war effort, received the following brief note from an Air Commodore Saunders:

"Dear Madam,

It is my painful duty to confirm the death of your husband, No.1375369 Sergeant Sidney Albert Peters of 50 Squadron, Royal Air Force, who was killed at 8.38 pm on the 21st January 1942, when the aircraft of which he was a member of the crew, crashed at the edge north of Peak Kinder Scout, Hayfield, Derbyshire, whilst engaged in air operations.

The Air Council desire to express their sympathy and deep regret at your husband's death in his Country's service."

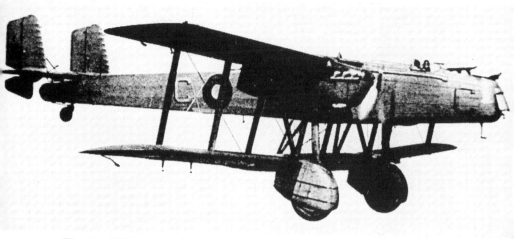

Heyford K6875, 166 Squadron, RAF, on a navigational night exercise from Leconfield, crashed Broadlee Bank Top, July 22nd, 1937.

Map reference 112862 ● Map key number 21

In 1936, November, 166 Squadron was re-formed as a heavy bomber squadron at Leconfield in Yorkshire and received the Handley Page Heyford, twin-engined, bomber. As the six-man crews trained to fly the ungainly aircraft it had already become obsolete. The biplane bomber's unconventional fixing of the fuselage to the upper wing, leaving a gap between it and the lower wing, gave the Heyford an ungainly appearance. The resulting distance from the ground of the cockpit did little to aid the pilot's view when landing. Nor did the open cockpit afford a practical 'office' from which to fly precision courses and navigate by night, in bad weather conditions — the co-pilot acting as navigator.

In December, 1936, six Heyfords in a flight of seven, from another squadron, 102 Squadron, force landed or crashed whilst on a flight from Northern Ireland to Finningley. The Heyfords had run into bad weather over the Pennines and

only one reached base. In the resulting forced landings and crashes three airmen lost their lives; it was the RAF's worst peacetime disaster (see Dark Peak Aircraft Wrecks, Book 2).

On the night of July 22nd, 1937, just seven months after the near annihilation of 102 Squadron's Heyfords over the Pennines, yet another Heyford found itself in trouble over the same area. Again the weather was atrocious but adding to the problem for the crew from 166 Squadron was darkness. At the controls was Sergeant Baker as the bomber flew low up Edale Valley with the crew desperately trying to make out some recognisable feature on the ground. The crew were on a night navigational exercise and were hoplessly lost in the murk. Flares were fired off by the crew to illuminate the ground beneath; the view of the terrain below must have puzzled the crew for it could not have been what they had expected to see — they were 13 miles off course.

Baker must have decided to drop down even lower, for a wing tip struck the high ground and the huge flying structure slewed round out of control, before smashing into the hilltop and bursting into flames.

Mr W. Dearnaly, who lived near the Nag's Head Inn at Edale, was in his bedroom at just gone 11 o'clock when he heard the sound of aero engines low overhead.

"It was so unusual here that I looked through the window and saw a huge machine just skimming over the top of Rushop Edge, heading for Kinder Scout. As it came to the edge of Grindlow there was a fearful crash and immediately flames shot up reddening the sky.

"I looked at my watch — the time was 17 minutes past 11. I dashed downstairs and collected a pick and shovel. Outside, other villagers were running towards the hill, some had an ambulance box and stretcher.

"In the dark we climbed as quickly as we could up the steep, rough path to the summit. We found a blazing furnace, which we approached with difficulty. We could see men's bodies in the flames but could not get near them for the heat. I dug loose earth and we threw it onto the wreckage to damp the flames."

In the valley of Edale, in the pre-war days, there was a camp for the unemployed and Mr Edwin Beeley, who was a member of the Committee of the Hyde League of Social Services, was visiting. He was standing outside a marquee with the unemployed centre supervisor when he heard the aircraft pass overhead in the darkness.

"A short time after it had passed over I heard a crash and saw flames on the mountain top. I realised that the plane had come to grief, and so I asked if there was anyone willing to accompany me to the top. Five men went with me and we took with us a stretcher and an ambulance box. We did not follow the ordinary path, but made a beeline up the mountainside and it was hard going.

"When we reached the plane after about an hour, we saw that the occupants were past our aid and so we waited until the police arrived later.

"We did not know what kind of plane it was until someone picked up a half burnt piece of paper bearing the letters 'RAF' and handed it to the police.

"It was a terrible sight for my first visit to the camp and I hope that I never see anything like it again."

In the darkness and frequent showers of rain, men went stumbling over the rough, slippery hilltop looking vainly for any occupant of the plane who might have been thrown clear of the main wreckage.

With the first light of dawn the appalling nature of the crash could be fully appreciated. The Heyford had struck the slope some 50 feet below the summit of the hill, ripping through the undergrowth, gouging a pit in the black earth, before smashing through a dry stone wall. Pieces of wreckage had been flung 50 feet ahead of the final resting place of the twisted and blackened air frame that had once been an RAF bomber.

It must have burst into flames upon impact with the ground and burnt with such ferocity that within minutes it had been reduced to a tangled mass of metal. Four of the crew lay close together with their arms thrown up in front of their faces as if to protect themselves. Two more bodies were located a little clear of the wreckage — all were badly burnt, almost beyond human recognition.

When it was realised, in the cold light of day, that there was nothing that could be done the police mounted a guard all around the wreckage so that nothing could be touched. A crash squad from the aerodrome at Hucknall arrived to take

Above: *Newspaper photograph taken the day after the accident.*

Above: **McDonald,** *sixth from the left, standing.*

Left: **Harry Grey,** *at the front kneeling.*

charge pending expert examination by Air Ministry officials.

The crew of six consisted of:

Sergeant Baker, pilot, from Thetford, Norfolk; Sergeant McMillan, co-pilot from London; Sergeant Barker from Beverley, Yorkshire; Aircraftman Eric McDonald, from Liverpool; Aircraftman Grey, wireless operator from Aberdare; Aircraftman Musker from Liverpool.

Heyford K6875, when it was issued to the Squadron, had been allocated to a certain Pilot Officer D. M. Strong and consequently it was he who was responsible for keeping an inventory of all the equipment on it. Although an officer, he normally flew as second pilot to Sergeant Baker, however, because he had crossed swords with the flight commander, he had been given other duties. On the evening of the fateful night exercise, Pilot Officer Strong found himself acting as the aerodrome control pilot and Sergeant McMillan had taken his place on board K6875. Strong survived the war and retired as an air commodore.

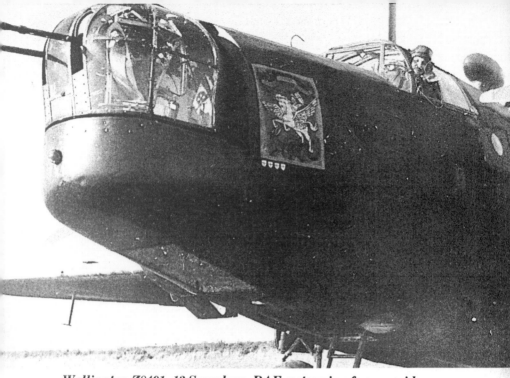

Wellington Z8491, 12 Squadron, RAF, returning from a raid, crashed White Edge Moor, February 6th, 1942.

Map reference 270770 ● Map key number 22

Prior to them crashing in deep snow close by a reservoir near Sheffield, that particular crew of 12 Squadron had set a record for one engine flying by a two-engined bomber. That feat carried out on October 13th, 1941 earned for the pilot the Distinguished Flying Cross.

On that particular occasion they had been briefed for an attack on the marshalling yards at Nurnberg. They were carrying three 500 lb bombs three 250 lb bombs and six small bomb containers as they lifted off the runway at Binbrook in Lincolnshire. It was 7 o'clock and growing dark as they climbed into the clear skies and turned on a southerly heading.

All went well so far and once over the target, at a height of 16,500 feet they released their bombs and began their turn for base. It was at that point that

Pilot Officer Colin Barnes noticed a sudden temperature rise in the starboard engine — the needle on the cylinder head temperature dial continued to climb alarmingly. Turning the aircraft well away from the probing fingers of the searchlights, Barnes attempted to lower the temperature on the defective engine by throttling back. The temperature, however, continued to rise and there was the real danger of fire. There was nothing for it but to switch off the engine and feather the propellor.

In view of the extreme distance from England the possibility of heading for Switzerland was considered by the 'Skipper'. But, to his annoyance, he learned that his navigator had not brought along any of the charts necessary to plot a course to that neutral

Above: *(left to right) 'Kit' Carson, wireless operator; Brian Lunn, air gunner; Colin Barnes, pilot; Bob Coldwell, navigator; Johnny Blute, air gunner; unnamed crew member.*

country. There seemed little alternative to attempting the long haul back nursing the Wellington along on one good engine. A wireless transmission was sent back to base informing them of the engine failure. That was the last message that they were able to send. It was the now dead starboard engine which produced the power for the generator, which in turn powered the wireless transmitter. Losing it meant no radio — and no heaters for the crew.

If they were going to make it back they would have to lighten the aircraft, and the crew set about jettisoning all removable equipment. Even the two machine guns in the front turret were taken out and dismantled before being launched from the struggling bomber. The two machine guns in the rear turret were retained in case of a beam attack by a night fighter. Petrol cocks were adjusted so as to first use up fuel in the starboard tanks, thus lightening that wing and helping the overall trim.

After what seemed like an eternity to the anxious crew, whose full attention was centred on the performance of the good engine, the navigator announced that they should be over the English coast. Sergeant Coldwell calculated that they had made landfall over the Lincolnshire coast and he gave the Skipper a course change that should put them in line for Binbrook. Letting down through the cloud they spotted the flashing identification code of an airfield — it was Tangmere, a fighter field in the south of England. It would have to do, they were just glad to be home and Coldwell was immediately forgiven by the crew. A hundred miles or so out in the circumstances wasn't all that bad. The Skipper, Colin Barnes wasn't so sure.

Control at Tangmere could not be contacted and there was no question of doing circuits before landing, or of having another go once they had lost height, for there was not enough power — it had to be right first time.

Pilot Officer Colin Barnes lined up the runway and pulled off a classic landing. A record had been set for making the longest flight by a twin-engined bomber flying on one engine whilst on operations. Over 550 miles, much of it over enemy territory and they were all back safe. An official communique commented upon the skill of Colin

Flew 550 miles with 'dead' wing

THE pilot of a Wellington bomber has set up a record by bringing his aircraft safely home from Bavaria—a distance of 550 miles—on one engine.

The raid had been on Nuremberg and the Wellington had unloaded its bombs. Then, suddenly, the starboard engine failed.

For hours the pilot—most of the time over hostile country in thick cloud—fought to keep the "dead" wing up.

"We jettisoned everything we could spare, down the flare-chute, to lighten the aircraft," he says.

"My second pilot, a New Zealander, took the front guns to bits and scattered them piecemeal along our track.

Jettisoned

"We sent one 'Trying to make base' radio message in code. After that the radio failed and we had to depend entirely on navigation.

"When we jettisoned the oxygen bottles it was a bit of a job cutting steel netting and tubes with an axe. But down the chute they went.

"Our track should have brought us out on the Dutch coast, but actually we must have crossed further south. There was about ten tenths cloud and steering was not very easy.

"I can tell you I was pleased to see a flare-path waiting for us. I sent every one back to brace themselves for a rough landing since I knew I'd have only one shot with one engine.

"But there was no trouble. Two nights later I was out again."

CRIPPLED BOMBER

FLIES 550 MILES HOME ON ONE ENGINE

The pilot of a Wellington bomber has set up a record by bringing it home 550 miles from Bavaria on one engine.

It happened after a big raid on Nuremberg. After the Wellington had unloaded its bombs, the starboard engine failed, and the pilot set off home with crew jettisoning machine-guns part by part, oxygen bottles, and everything they could spare to lighten the plane.

As the pilot fought all the time to keep the "dead" wing up, the bomber droned onwards over hostile country in thick cloud. Back over Britain, he landed "without trouble" after eight hours' continuous flying.

This is claimed as the longest distance covered by a two-engined bomber with one of its engines dead.

D.F.C. for Gallantry

Pilot Officer Colin Arthur Barnes, of the R.A.F. Volunteer Reserve, whose home is in Beckenham, has been awarded the Distinguished Flying Cross. He has carried out sorties over heavily defended targets with skill and determination, and on numerous occasions has remained in heavy concentrations while making several runs over the target. He is a fine operational pilot and captain of aircraft.

118

Above: *Colin Barnes wrote concerning the crew badge; "I designed a crest and my wireless operator very cleverly drew and painted it on the nose of the kite. It is a winged horse with St George killing the Nazi dragon and holding the crusaders' shield. Above is the old school motto, 'Domine Dirgige Nos', 'O Lord Direct Us', which is a hint to the navigator."*

Barnes: 'His skilful piloting, cool judgement, superb captaincy and airmanship'. It went on to say how those qualities had inspired a high standard of morale in his crew. It is known that his crew had the highest regard for him and were very sorry when a crash in the Peak District split them up just four months after that epic flight.

On the night of February 6th, 1942, at around 5.30, eight aircraft of 12 Squadron and five aircraft of 142 Squadron took off from Grimsby. They were detailed to carry out a raid on the French port of Brest. In the event, ten aircraft arrived over the Atlantic port at spaced intervals only to find the target obscured by cloud. There could be no question of bombing blind as it could have meant French civilians being the victims. Like the other bomber crews, the crew of Wellington Z8491 turned for

home with their bombs still on board.

Following the course corrections given to him by his navigator, Sergeant Coldwell, Colin Barnes gently nosed down through clouds heavy with snow. They were over the flat Lincolnshire countryside and on course for Binbrook — or so they thought. Wellington Z8491 smacked onto White Edge at 200 miles an hour, coming from a south westerly direction, impacting just above the top of the Edge. Helped by the thick layer of snow, the aircraft bounced and slithered across the flat moorland. When the bomber first struck the ground, co-pilot Jack Seamen was catapulted out through a hatch and flung into a deep snow drift.

The bomber came to rest with its back broken and the rear section twisted over. Somehow the crash failed to detonate the seven 500 lb bombs, and there was

Above: *A painting of the final position of Z8491, painted by Kit Carson.*
Opposite right: **Pilot Officer Colin Barnes.**

no fire. A shaken Colin Barnes was still in his seat wondering what had happened, blood from a gash in his forehead streaming down his face; one of his ankles was broken. There should have been sufficient height according to the altimeter. They were 60 miles off course and consequently, instead of the flat Lincolnshire countryside they were over the Pennine mountains — another navigational error of some significance.

The navigator, Bob Coldwell and wireless operator, 'Kit' Carson had both escaped with minor injuries and they were able to extract their Skipper from the pilot's seat. Bomb aimer, Brian Lunn had been in the front turret and was badly concussed and injured. Wireless operator, Kit Carson had been away from his crew position when the bomber struck the moor. He had gone back down the fuselage to change the recognition flares, since it had gone beyond midnight and the colour recognition had changed. He noted that the wireless operator's position had suffered heavy damage, being twisted and crushed — he had had a narrow escape.

Coldwell and Carson crawled up through the rear section to the tail gunner's position and there they found Johnny Blute hanging upside down. He was trapped by an iron bar and no matter how they pulled and tugged they were unable to free him. Other than being upside down and firmly trapped he was otherwise all right. Of the co-pilot, Jack Seamen, there was no trace — as far as they could see he had simply vanished.

When Jack Seamen had sufficiently recovered to take stock of his situation he decided that somehow he was in occupied France, and he ought to be taking steps to avoid being picked up by the Germans. The swirling snow hid the position of the Wellington from him and he staggered off to try and find

somewhere to hide until daybreak, then he would contact the local resistance group.

Back at the aircraft it was decided who should go and raise the alarm. Coldwell complained of a pain in his groin and so it was left to Kit Carson to try and fetch help. He set off in what he hoped would be the right direction and ended up crossing the frozen surface of Barbrook Reservoir. Without realising it he was heading towards grave danger for the ice close to the towers had been broken up.

Water Board worker, Mr Sayles, had been out earlier that night to stoke up the brazier positioned in the reservoir tunnel to prevent an outlet pipe freezing up. As he was leaving and heading back towards his house he thought that he heard a crashing sound up on the moor.

"I stood listening for a minute or two, then I thought that I heard what sounded like shouting. After that there was silence — no sound at all anywhere."

Later that night, at around midnight, Mr and Mrs Sayles were standing at their door looking out into the darkness. Quite clearly they heard shouts for help and they could see a light moving along

SIGNAL FROM GROUP
or
How it appears to us

The day dawns warm and sunny,
The forecast - clear and bright,
Although this may sound funny
There'll be no "ops" tonight

An Air-Vice-Marshall, by his fire,
Looks out one foggy morn,
Runways thick with mud and mire
And a bloody great thunderstorm

He rubbed his hands with a fiendish sneer,
From his eyes shone a baleful light,
He shook with glee, and was, I fear,
A really most horrid sight

He woke his minions from their sleep
And from the carpet took a bite
"There's rain and hail and snow and sleet,"
"BINBROOK FLIES TONIGHT!"

An anonymous member of 12 Squadron

the reservoir wall. They called out to the figure to stay where he was as he was in danger of falling at that section of the wall.

Sergeant Kit Carson had at last reached help and was taken into the house. However, the waterman viewed him with deep suspicion. Mr Sayles whispered to his wife to be ready to hit the visitor over the head with a poker if he tried to move from the chair where he had slumped. Meanwhile, he would run off to raise the alarm with the local Home Guard unit. Upon returning with the soldiers and satisfying himself that the young man was who he said he was, and not an enemy agent intent on mischief, he set off up the moor with a storm lantern. Some of the fitter members of the Home Guard followed him.

"I arrived at the site and could see that the bomber had hit a bump, jumped, landed again and then slewed round. The back end of the tail had twisted and the tail gunner was trapped upside down in his turret. There was a bomb at the side of the plane and near it was an injured crewman. The pilot and the front gunner were both unconscious."

Mr Sayles half carried Bob Coldwell back down the moor leaving the Home Guard to make the others as comfortable as possible. As Mr Sayles went off into the night with his burden, one of the old soldiers took off his greatcoat and wrapped it around one of the injured men. Because of that kind act the soldier began to suffer from exposure. He was later to die as a direct result of illness caused by his night out on the moor.

By the time that Mr Sayles had got back to the house with Coldwell the police had arrived. Whereupon the police sergeant ordered Mr Sayles to lead them back up the moor, and he said that Sayles should have waited for them to arrive before going up with elements of the Home Guard. Exhausted from half

Above: *Jack Seamen*

carrying and half dragging the injured navigator to safety, Mr Sayles was in no mood to be spoken to like a naughty boy and flatly refused to budge until he had recovered. The next to arrive at the house was a doctor and some RAF personnel commanded by an officer. Mr Sayles was ready to lead a party up the moor again.

Johnny Blute, hanging upside down in his turret, was given a shot of morphine, and then began the job of cutting him out. By the dawn light they had him free and onto a stretcher — he had been trapped for twelve hours.

As for Jack Seamen, who had been

convinced that he was somewhere in France, he was found later that morning suffering from frostbite and cracked ribs. He was later to lose some fingers when they failed to recover from frostbite.

The crash on White Edge Moor was the end for that particular crew, for they broke up and went to other assignments. Pilot Officer Colin Barnes, DFC, never flew on missions again, although he did fly on many occasions as an instructor with various Heavy Conversion Units, training bomber crews. He finished his war service with the rank of Squadron Leader and died in April, 1983. Brian Lunn, after he had recovered, joined another crew and was posted 'missing in action' in September, 1942. Johnny Blute, the rear gunner, was killed on a bombing mission, April, 1944. Co-pilot, Jack Seamen, survived the war and died recently. Wireless operator, 'Kit' Carson, also survived and is believed to be living somewhere in Leeds.

Bob Coldwell must have honed up his skills as a navigator, perhaps helped by bitter experience, for he was eventually posted to a Pathfinder squadron, much to the puzzlement of his one-time skipper, Colin Barnes, who had a low opinion of his navigating skills. Flight Lieutenant Robert Coldwell, DSO, DFM, of the Pathfinder Force, failed to return from a bombing raid in May, 1944.

Below: *After the war Pilot Officer Colin Barnes returned to the crash site with his wife and took this photograph. Mrs Barnes is standing on the site of the crash; Barbrook Reservoir can be seen in the background.*

Dragon Rapide G-ALBC, Solair Flying Services, returning from a photographic assignment, crashed Kinder Scout, December 30th, 1963.

Map reference 102883 • Map key number 23

The de Havilland DH89 Dragon Rapide airliner was one of the all-time classics among aircraft, for it played a vital part in the beginnings of civil aviation history and the type was still operating until recent times. In those early days of commercial aviation it made economical sense to operate the twin-engined Rapide.

With the outbreak of the Second World War the DH89 had a second lease of life when the RAF bought several hundred to use in a light transport role. Then in the immediate post war period surplus Rapides were sold off to emerging airlines. It was the jet powered commercial aircraft which saw off the Rapide and relegated it to pleasure and charter work. During the sixties it was being used by parachutists for pleasure jumps. In the next decade there was a surge of interest in historical aviation and, despite the lack of spares, the Rapide became a much sought after type. The 'Gentleman's Carriage', as it was referred to, presented exactly the right image for enthusiasts keen on nostalgia. It was an aircraft of the thirties with its fixed undercarriage — more importantly, it was a biplane. It could carry passengers, paying joyriders if needs be, and it was economical to operate. A truly popular aircraft with some sixty or more still around after half a century (it was built in 1934) — many of them are still in flying condition.

The remains of a Dragon Rapide lay scattered about at a spot on Kinder Scout. It represents the last aircraft type to fall foul of that part of the Pennine Mountains known as the 'Dark Peak'.

Above: *Dragon Rapide G-ALBC, from a colour snap taken by a hill walker before it was broken up and burnt. Some wooden spars and remnants of the engines litter the site today.*

Dragon Rapide G-ALBC of Solair Flying Services was returning from Middleton St George, near Darlington, to Birmingham after carrying out a photographic survey flight. The pilot, Captain Dennis Holmes, decided to divert to Manchester to refuel. His co-pilot was twenty years old John McWhirter; he had been at the controls earlier but after handing back control to Holmes, he was resting.

He must have fallen asleep, for the next thing he remembered was being flung through the air and landing amongst moorland peat. Shakily, he crawled back to the crumpled wreckage that had so recently been an aeroplane

where he was able to locate Dennis Holmes. He was relieved to find Holmes alive but in great pain from a broken leg. After much tugging and struggling he managed to pull Holmes free from the tangled mess, whereupon he tied up the injured limb as best he could. What should they do next? Should they attempt to walk off the moor to raise the alarm, or stay with the aircraft in the hope that searchers would find them quickly?

With the aircraft being overdue the Mountain Rescue Services were alerted and around fifty men began to comb the moors. However, it was a helicopter that spotted the broken Rapide and shortly

after that, as darkness fell, rescuers located the two men huddled together to keep warm.

Young John McWhirter was taken off the moor first by way of Edale, where an ambulance was waiting to take him to Stockport Infirmary. It was a more difficult job for the stretcher party to carry Dennis Holmes five miles off a moor laced with bogs and mud on a bitterly cold December night.

Captain Holmes expressed the opinion that the aircraft had been caught in a sudden downdraught — they had been warned of turbulence over the Pennines earlier.

Below: *Author Ron Collier at the wreck site in the early '80s with some of the Dragon Rapide fragments.*

Dakota G-AHCY, BEA, on a passenger flight from Belfast to Manchester, crashed Wimberry Stones, August 19th, 1949.

Map reference 014025 ● Map key number 24

If you had ever been convinced that you had carried out a certain task or action, only to find later that you only thought that you had, it can be disturbing — it is rarely fatal. When a person is responsible for the lives of others and he suffers a lapse of that sort it can result in tragedy. That was the case for the crew of three along with the twenty-one passengers of Dakota G-AHCY belonging to British European Airways Corporation. It was Friday, August 19th, 1949; First Officer Gordon Holt sought out the Meteorological Officer at Nutts Corner, Belfast. What was the weather like over the Irish Sea and particularly around Ringway, Manchester? He was shown that morning's weather chart and given the forecast. It was cloudy over western England, but the conditions were such as not to cause undue delay for the twenty nine holiday makers who had booked a flight on the ex-RAF DC3, Dakota.

Before being acquired by BEA in 1946 it had been refurbished by the Scottish Motor Traction Company, to carry passengers. The aircraft had completed 1,256 flying hours with the RAF and since it received its civilian Certificate of Registration it had continuously held a Certificate of Airworthiness.

At 10.58 "Charlie Yoke" (last two registration letters of G-AHCY) was airborne, just eight minutes behind schedule. The pilot, Captain Frank Pinkerton, set course 118 degrees and the First Officer entered the course change in the log book. Because of the cloud overcast at Ringway, Manchester, Instrument Flight Rules were in force — that was confirmed over the radio transmitter from Ringway. Upon reaching 5,500 feet the airliner levelled off and maintained a ground speed of about 170 knots. In just over one hour they would be touching down at Ringway. The aircraft was slightly off-course by a few degrees north of the flight path. A check was made on GEE equipment (Radar position finding apparatus) on the airliner which confirmed that they were too far north.

In order to put the aircraft back on course a turn of seven degrees to starboard was required. One of the crew entered that seven degree turn in the log — but the actual manoeuvre was never

Above: *After the war DC3s were converted from their military role and fitted out to take around thirty passengers. Most postwar emerging airlines equipped themselves with the Dakota.*

carried out. Charlie Yoke was on course for the 1,500 feet high Pennine mountains. Captain Pinkerton must have thought that he had carried out the turn. He was an experienced pilot, having flown 2,300 hours by day and 1,091 hours by night. He was regularly on the Belfast - Manchester route and had flown into Ringway some 88 times in two years.

Instrument flight rules were in force at Ringway because of the overcast and the Standard Beam Approach system was in operation. The system consisted of a radio beacon transmitting morse signals continuously — the letters 'A' and 'N'. Only 'A's were heard by the aircraft's crew on one side of the intended line of approach, and only 'N's on the other. By that method an aircraft picking up the signals could ascertain in which direction the airfield lay. Directly over the main radio beacon there was no signal at all — it was known as the 'Cone of Silence'. Once the signals stopped the pilot knew that he was directly over the airfield, even though he had no sight of the ground.

"Charlie Yoke approaching from the northwest at 3,500 feet, descending to 1,500 feet, flying under I.F.R. E.T.A. 11.57. — Over!"

Charlie Yoke was calling Ringway Air Traffic Control.

"You are clear for S.B.A. approach at 1,500 feet, call at main beacon, runway clear. Over!"

"Message understood, will report over main beacon. What is the cloud base? — Over!"

"Ringway control to Charlie Yoke, cloud base 8/8ths at 1,200 feet, aircraft say 600. — Over!"

The message was acknowledged and some minutes passed by before the controller at Ringway called for Charlie Yoke's present position, as he had another aircraft waiting to take off.

Following that message Charlie Yoke requested a QDM (compass bearing) and a reply was sent giving 242 degrees Magnetic. The QDM was acknowledged by the aircraft and a statement was sent, "Passed field on QDR." Herein lies a mystery, what led the crew to believe that they were over the cone of silence? The Dakota's position had been fixed with some certainty by GEE and in the time given it was not possible for Charlie Yoke to have passed over Ringway, it was about twelve miles to the north east. Had there been a fading of the beam causing the crew to draw the wrong conclusion? That theory was finally discarded by a court of inquiry when evidence was taken from witnesses who had themselves experienced fading by the Ringway beam. They all agreed that fading could never be mistaken for the cone of silence, and it was therefore most unlikely that Captain Pinkerton had been misled as to his actual position in that way. The explanation was given that the message had probably been misunderstood and that the crew were really saying that they were 'progressing to the airfield and QDR' rather than 'passing the airfield on QDR'.

In order for the aircraft to line up with the runway it would have to make a 315 degree turn. Pinkerton was convinced that he was in the correct position to

Captain Frank Whartley Pinkerton
During the war he served as a sergeant pilot in the RAF and was posted missing believed killed when his bomber was shot down in 1942. However, he had successfully baled out and was helped by the Dutch underground movement to escape. He was passed from one escape unit to another, walking for most of the way through Belgium and France. He crossed the Pyrenees into Spain where he was interned for a short time. Upon his release he returned to England and took up operational duties in the RAF once again. He completed his war service with a commisssion and went on to take up a career in civil aviation with British European Airways.

Frank Pinkerton was a local man in that he was born and raised in Hyde. Prior to the war he been had been employed at ICI (Leathercloth Division) Ltd, Newton. By coincidence, the very area of the crash at Chew Valley, had been a favourite hiking ground for him in the pre-war days.

He had married during the war and had a three year old son. His home at the time of the accident was at Wallasey.

execute the required turn — it was 11.59.

Continued on page 134

"This is Charlie Yoke to Ringway, making procedure turn now. — Over!"

"Ringway to Charlie Yoke . . . Call outer marker QDM. QFE 1017 mbs. You are Number One clear to approach. — Over!"

After Ringway Air Traffic Control had informed the crew of the QFE at Ringway (barometric pressure at aerodrome level) and that Number One runway was clear for their use, there was no further contact.

Captain Pinkerton, believing his position to be fifteen miles southwest of where he actually was, called for the undercarriage to be lowered. Easing the throttles back he proceeded to nose down through the clouds.

The sound of a low flying aircraft caused farmer, Mr T. Buckley, who was working in his field, to glance up. The moors rose steeply to a mist clad mountain 1,500 feet high which loomed over and dominated his land. The aeroplane was not in sight but it sounded dangerously low; then he heard an almighty crash followed by silence.

Racing up the bracken covered slope he was joined by another farmer, Mr H. Walker. Together they toiled up to the scene of the wreck, and came upon the shattered airliner. There were flames shooting up from twisted metal and bodies along with items of luggage were strewn all around. Between them they managed to free one woman who was trapped in the wreckage, with tongues of fire sweeping towards her. As it happened, she was not too badly injured. There followed two small explosions as broken fuel tanks ignited. A small boy was carried out of the twisted metal shards, shaken but alive — his parents had also survived but his brother had been killed.

Many local people began to arrive on the scene as did workers from Greenfield Mill, making the two mile climb to assist the injured. Down at the mill doctors, the ambulance and fire services were being telephoned and the canteen was being prepared as a base for use by the rescuers. All the injured passengers were strapped to stretchers and carried by up to eight or even ten men down the mountainside. The dead were left until last and were taken to the mortuary at Uppermill. Of the twenty nine passengers and three crew, just eight passengers had survived. Captain Pinkerton's body was the last one to be removed from the wreckage, his watch having stopped at 1.02 (British Summer Time) two minutes past twelve.

Opposite: *The official explanation as to what must have occured, indicating that a course correction entered in the aircraft's log was not executed by the pilot.*

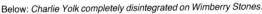

Below: *Charlie Yolk completely disintegrated on Wimberry Stones.*

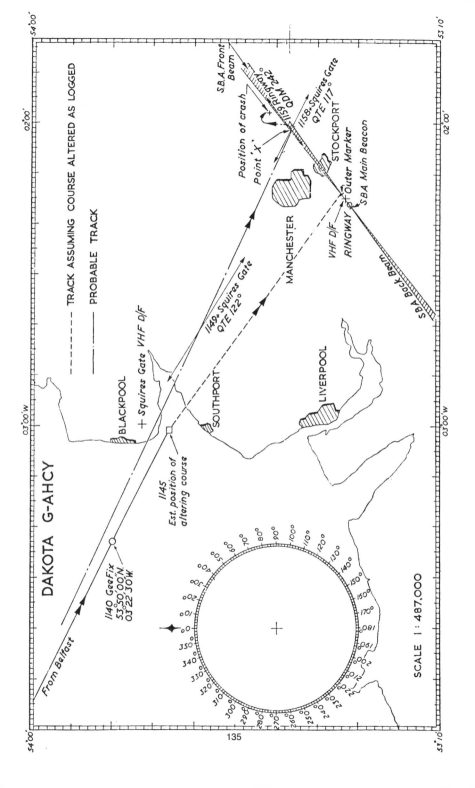

DAKOTA G-AHCY

SCALE 1 : 487,000

----- TRACK ASSUMING COURSE ALTERED AS LOGGED
——— PROBABLE TRACK

From Belfast

1140 GeeFix
53°50'00"N.
03°22'30"W.

1145
Est. position of
altering course

+ Squires Gate VHF D/F

BLACKPOOL

SOUTHPORT

1149+ Squires Gate
QTE 122°

LIVERPOOL

MANCHESTER

Position of crash
Point 'X'

S.B.A. Front
Beam

QDM 242°
QND 062°
1159 QDM 242°

1158+ Squires Gate
QTE 117°

STOCKPORT

VHF D/F
RINGWAY Outer Marker

S.B.A Main Beacon

S.B.A. Back Beam

0°
10°
20°
30°
40°
50°
60°
70°
80°
90°
100°
110°
120°
130°
140°
150°
160°
170°
180°
190°
200°
210°
220°
230°
240°
250°
260°
270°
280°
290°
300°
310°
320°
330°
340°
350°

This page and opposite: *Searching and caring for survivors.*

What was the cause of the accident? A Court of Investigation, after carefully considering all the evidence, made its report the following year to the Minister of Civil Aviation. They had found that on the aircraft's departure from Ireland it was in good condition and that the engines were operating well. Also they found that the radio equipment was functioning properly. Also that there was no gale force winds or violent storms that could have caused the accident. Air Traffic Control officers at Ringway were found to be operating the control system

correctly and in accordance with regulations laid down.

The Court of Investigation regretfully came to the conclusion that human error in failing to make the course alteration of seven degrees to starboard, as entered in the log, was the direct cause of the accident. Also that over confidence on the part of the pilot in his navigation had led him to make a wrong assumption, in that when he commenced his procedure turn, he was nearer to the airport than he actually was. The pilot had failed to carry out the correct procedure when making his Standard Beam Approach, in that he did not fly over the cone of silence before commencing his let down.

The point of impact of Dakota G-AHCY was at the head of a ravine on Wimberry Rocks, about eighty yards from the top of the mountain.

Mosquito PF395, 571 Squadron, RAF, Fast Night Striking Force, returning from a raid on Hamburg, crashed Dean Rocks, Chew Valley, October 22nd, 1944.

Map reference 026032 ● Map key number 25

The Fast Night Striking Force had been brought into existence to cause disruption in the lives of the German populace. From 1944 Mosquito aircraft ranged across Germany dropping their small bomb loads on widely spaced targets, causing the sirens to be sounded throughout the land — these were dubbed 'Siren Tours'. Factory workers were kept hurrying to the shelters, their sleep suffered and so did their work output. The F.N.S.F. was also employed ahead of the main Pathfinder crews to drop 'Window' to confuse the German radar, or to carry out what was known as 'spoof' raids; the intention being, to get the Luftwaffe air defence controllers to commit their nightfighters to the wrong city, leaving the main bomber force with just the flak defences to contend with.

That special force operated with the highly successful Mosquito MkXVI with its enlarged bomb bay, which took one 4,000 lb blast bomb, known affectionately as a 'Cookie'.

One squadron in that special force was 571 Squadron, which had been formed in April, 1944 and was part of 8 Group,

Pathfinder Force. It was an aircraft of that Squadron which flew into Dean Rocks, Dove Stones, on the evening of October 22nd, 1944, killing the pilot and navigator.

The crews had been briefed for a raid on the much battered city of Hamburg, but because of bad weather conditions, the mission was cancelled. Again, the following day, crews of twelve bombed up Mosquitos climbed into their flying gear and waited for the word to go — but yet again they had to stand down. On the following day, the 22nd, the crews prepared for the raid and on that occasion they were cleared to go. Eleven aircraft took off at one minute intervals each carrying a single blast bomb — it was around 5 o'clock when they began taking off. In order not to give the enemy a clear radar picture of their intentions and possible destination, the Mosquitos of 571 Squadron zig-zagged across the North Sea.

The city of Hamburg had 'died' the previous year when it was constantly bombed for three nights. Huge fire storms were created by the bombing and swept through the heart of the city consuming all before. Over 6,000 acres in the most densely packed and ancient part of the city had been razed to the ground. It had been the worst bombing disaster up until that time. All work at Hamburg's four main shipbuilding yards had been severely curtailed. The city was still considered a worthwhile target in October 1944.

The raiders were over Hamburg at 6.40 as darkness fell, the city being easily located on the H2S screen — a navigational aid carried in the leading aircraft. At 6.45, individual aircraft of 571 Squadron dropped beneath the ten tenths cloud cover at 10,000 feet and the navigators sought out the red and green target indicators dropped by the leading Pathfinder Mosquito. In turn each raider picked out the more accurately placed red marker flares and released their deadly cargoes, before turning for home. Flak burst ever closer to the speeding planes as the anti-aircraft gunners tried to get their height and speed. As the Mosquitos winged out over the North Sea some of the crews reported seeing a tremendous explosion on the ground, no doubt set off by their attack. Some success, and so far without loss to themselves.

Once clear of the bursting anti aircraft fire, heaviest to the north of Hamburg, the pilots and navigators set course for home, which for them was Oakington, in Cambridgeshire. By 8.30 they would all be safely on the ground at de-briefing — and after that, no doubt a welcome pint for most of them. There was still danger from nightfighters; some enemy pilot might try his luck at intercepting the fleeing bombers as they sped first northward and then to the West. The plywood built Mosquito was fast when fully weighted with fuel and bomb load, it was virtually impossible to catch when lightened. The new jet powered Me262

could match it, but there was none around that night. A single engined enemy fighter was spotted by two Mosquito crews, attempting the chase, but it was shown a clean pair of heels.

It was shortly after the first course change that Mosquito PF395, piloted by Flying Officer Douglas Scotland, experienced problems. There was a drastic fall in the rev counter for the port engine and subsequent loss of power. The reason was seen in the stream of white-grey vapour pouring from the exhaust stubs, glycol coolant under pressure was getting into the cylinders — the cylinder head gasket had blown. With the oil temperature gauge climbing rapidly, Doug Scotland throttled back on the port engine, threw the ignition switch and feathered the propellor.

The navigator, Sergeant Humphrey Soan, called up the crew of one of the other aircraft in the vicinity and told them of their problem — that they would be late home for supper. The 'Mossy' flew well enough on one engine and there was little likelihood of running into an enemy fighter so close to the English coast.

Mosquito PF395 was alone and losing height gradually, but there would have been no undue concern on the part of Scotland and Soan. There was plenty of power in the starboard Rolls-Royce Merlin power plant and the aircraft could be easily landed on one engine.

The real problem for the two-man crew was the loss of radio and other navigational aids, brought about when the port engine stopped. It was that engine which packed power into the generator and cockpit cabin super-charger. Shortly they were flying blind and too far north, missing their base at Oakington, near Cambridge, by some sixty miles.

Hopelessly lost over northern England and the Pennine mountain chain, the Mosquito began circling as Scotland and

Above: *Flying Officer Douglas Scotland*

Soan peered at the ground looking for landmarks. At the town of Dukinfield, near the hills , two young brothers were roused from their beds by the sound of a low flying aircraft.

"We looked out of the bedroom window, but at first we couldn't see a thing, then we spotted a light flashing," recalled one of them later.

In the nose of the Mosquito, Sergeant Soan was working an Aldis signalling lamp, flashing Morse, hoping for some response from the ground. Scotland was turning the aircraft in an anti clockwise circle and was banking around the house where the two boys watched helplessly. The youngest implored the older to reply using their father's torch. After all, he had once boasted that he could receive and send Morse messages. However, faced with that very real situation, the older lad had to admit that he had been spinning a line.

"If only one of us could have understood Morse code, we may have saved two lives that night."

Unable to get any response, Duggie Scotland, straightened the Mossy and headed eastwards. They must have considered baling out as an alternative to

Below: *Oxygen control panel from Mosquito PF395, now in Manchester Aerospace Museum.*

Above: *Sergeant Humphrey Soan*

locating an airfield on that dark, cloud filled night.

At twenty three minutes past 9 o'clock, about one hour after the other ten bombers had landed safely at Oakington, Mosquito PF395 flew into the hillside at Dove Stones, at the mouth of Chew Valley.

Scotland, prior to the war, had been a keen sportsman, playing tennis and football — he played in the first team of the London Caledonians. Prior to joining the RAF in 1941, he had been employed as a junior buyer with the Gas Company. In the RAF he had served for a time as an instructor and was experienced on the Mosquito, having logged 61 hours on the type. He left a wife and two children.

Before being called up, Humphrey Rupert Cruse Soan had worked on his father's farm at Battle in Sussex. When he was killed he was 22 years old and unmarried. In recent years he had eventually stopped growing and had reached a height of six feet five inches, a shy awkward youth who had filled out with a new found confidence during his training as a navigator in Canada. He joined the newly formed Fast Night Striking Force in 1944 where he was teamed up with Duggie Scotland.

Today very little remains at the crash site apart from some pieces of armour plating. The two men, Douglas Scotland and Humphrey Soan, are buried at Blacon Cemetery, Chester.

Below: *Sheets of armour plating and fragments of engine mounting frame below the site of the crash.*

Liberator B-24J, 42-52003, USAAF, 310 Ferring Squadron, on a delivery flight to Hardwick, crashed on Mill Hill, October 11th, 1944.

Map reference 055906 ● Map key number 52

310th Ferrying Squadron was brought into existence (activated) October 1943, and Sergeant Jerome Najvar was amongst the enlisted men forming the initial strength of the newly formed unit. The Squadron, a part of the 27 Air Transport Group, was stationed at Warton, near the village of Freckleton, in Lancashire. Since the aerodrome had been handed over to the 8th USAAF in July 1943, it had become the second largest American maintenance base, after Burtonwood, in the European theatre of operations.

The purpose of the base was to carry out modifications, repairs and overhauls on every type of aircraft in the US inventory, as well as many British types. Flying personnel consisted mainly of pilots and engineers, who were called upon to ferry new and repaired aircraft to the American operational squadrons.

Sergeant Jerome Najvar was a flight engineer and he was involved in a flying accident whilst delivering a brand new B-24J bomber, in October 1944, the remains of which lie scattered amongst the peat bogs.

Back in the early days of its forming, the 310th Squadron experienced teeth-ing problems and the Engineering Section, to which Najvar belonged, was involved in some extensive maintenance work. Because there was a shortage of manpower, the engineers were called upon to maintain all the aircraft in transit and a shift system had to be introduced in order to cope. There was constant pressure to keep up with deliveries of aircraft and during the month following its formation, 310th Squadron managed to safely deliver 627 bombers and 554 fighters throughout the British Isles. With such intensive activity there were bound to be accidents and during November there were five, resulting in two fatalities. During those hectic first weeks 'Jerry' Najvar experienced his first close shave when on his first delivery flight to Burtonwood.

Prior to the trip to deliver a B-24, an engineer and a pilot instructor went up with Najvar and the delivery pilot to help them familiarise with the type. Upon landing from the training flight the instructors handed over the Liberator along with maps and written orders. They took off all right and were soon in the circuit over Burtonwood on their first ever delivery. The pilot lined up the runway, lost height and began to throttle back. To their alarm the nose of the aircraft dipped immediately — they were going to set down well before the runway threshold. Quickly the pilot opened the throttles and the bomber skimmed over the grassed area and onto the tarmac. Under full power the Liberator tore along using up the runway at a frightening pace until the throttles were cut back and the brakes applied hard. They pulled up with a few yards to spare and both sat looking at each other trying to figure out what had happened. Simply, the pilot had failed to call for 'quarter flaps' which would have given the aircraft more lift at low air speed. They were learning the hard way — by experience. Jerry Najvar, from that time on, always reminded the ferry pilots when on the final approach to use flaps, especially when ferrying a B-24. He was to criss-cross England as flight engineer and co-pilot many times during the remainder of 1943 and most of '44, prior to his crash on Mill Hill.

As the invasion of Europe loomed ever closer, security at the USAAF base was tightened. It was said at the time that 310 Ferrying Squadron had one of the worst records for circulating rumours in the whole USAAF. Personnel at 310 had access to the progress of the air war on a daily basis; they were able to observe and pass comment on most aspects of air operations, from new types of aircraft, to the rate of accidents caused during transitional training; to damage caused by enemy action both in the UK and suffered during sweeps and missions over occupied territory. A 'Don't Talk' campaign was launched in an attempt to curb the 'scuttlebuck'.

In the month of July, following the landings in Normandy, Jerry Najvar helped to ferry 32 bombers, sometimes two in one day, mainly Flying Fortresses and Liberators, to the various bomber squadrons in the 'Mighty Eighth'. One of

the ferry aircraft would pick the crews up, usually late at night, and taxi them back to Warton.

There was constant pressure to deliver the daily quota of aircraft whatever the weather conditions and during the month of August tragedy struck. A B-24 was attempting a landing at Warton during a thunderstorm, when it dropped from the sky onto Freckleton village school, killing 70 persons.

With the onset of Autumn the weather began to deteriorate and on the morning of October 11th Jerry Najvar found himself sat in the 'Ready Lounge', at Burtonwood which was crowded with pilots and engineers. Outside, a thick fog shrouded the airfield bringing visibility down to nil and conversation among the crews centered on the weather — even the birds were walking. Some were reading through pilots' and engineers' notes familiarising themselves with changes and modifications to aircraft types. If conditions didn't improve soon then delivery schedules would take a severe knock.

Suddenly an officer with a clipboard entered the crowded room and called out, 'Lieutenant Haopt!' In answer, an officer detached himself from the rest and called out 'here!' Next, the officer with the clipboard called, 'Sergeant Najvar!' The powers that be, had decided to get the 'show on the road' despite conditions — Najvar and his pilot were to be the first ones up. Jerry Najvar had never met 2nd Lieutenant Creighton Haopt before and as they moved to leave the room together he threw up a quick salute. Haopt returned the gesture and held out his hand, shaking Jerry's hand warmly. They had little time to get to know each other and could only exchange brief pleasantries as they sped through the grey, damp blanket in one of the station trucks.

They were to deliver a brand new

B-24J, to Hardwick, just South of Norwich — the home of 93 Bombardment Group. It was a replacement aircraft for one of the squadron's lead aircraft, having H2X bombing radar apparatus installed on board .

Both Haopt and Najvar began to carry out the pre-flight checks; Najvar did the external inspection looking over the tyres, landing gear, wheel wells, engines etc. After Haopt had checked the cockpit he requested taxiing instructions and the control tower gave them permission to take off. At that time the fog was so thick that they were unable to see from one set of runway lights to the next.

With the four engines roaring at full revolutions, Haopt released the brakes and the Liberator began to move into the grey wall. There was a distinct thump as the starboard wheel hit one of the runway lights, to be followed by another bang as the next light in line was smashed. Haopt had to make a decision; if he attempted to swing away from the line of lights he could run off the runway and end up anywhere, perhaps colliding with parked aircraft (bombers were nose to tail all around the field). If he carried on smacking the lights he could end up with a punctured tyre and that could well be disastrous. There was nothing for it, but to attempt to get airborne at once. With insufficient airspeed the Liberator lifted off for a short distance before falling back onto the runway. Haopt once again heaved back on the control column and once again the bomber flopped back onto the tarmac. At the third attempt they remained aloft — but only just. Because of the low airspeed the controls were sluggish and unresponsive. As speed gradually built up Haopt gained more control, but Najvar noticed that his pilot was over-correcting every move of the aircraft — it had been a shaky take-off, they nearly hadn't made it. Understandably, it was

Below: *Official photograph showing the throttle quadrant with the throttle controls wide open, confirming that the aircraft was under power when it crashed.*

showing in the way that Haopt was handling the ungainly monster once the immediate danger had passed.

Once they were clear of Burtonwood and on course for Norfolk, Haopt seemed to relax a little, so Jerry Najvar unbuckled his harness and leaving his seat, he went aft where he could get a good view of the underside of the wings. There didn't appear to be any structural damage, the landing gear had retracted neatly and the two inner engines seemed to be clear of problems. He couldn't vouch for the two outer engines, for the simple reason that he couldn't see them — the fog was far too thick.

Back in the cockpit once more Najvar gave the thumbs up sign to Haopt and proceded to take out and open up a map. He compared it to the compass bearing and noticed that they were on a direct line for the high ground.

"I checked the altimeter — it was indicating 1,500 feet — we were too low to clear the hills," recalled Jerry Najvar. "I jabbed my finger at the high ground shown on the map and read off the

elevation for that area. Then I indicated with my thumb that we had better get some height."

Haopt nodded as if he understood, but he made no attempt to climb the bomber to a safe height. Had he misunderstood Najvar's signal to gain height for a 'thumbs up, all's well' indication? Or perhaps he thought that there would be sufficient time to climb. Whatever the reason for inaction on the pilot's part, Najvar was growing more and more concerned as the minutes passed. He started peering out of the bulge in the perspex on the co-pilot's side of the cockpit.

Suddenly he saw something dark pass under the aircraft:

"I grabbed the control column and pulled back on it with all my strength — the pilot realised what I was doing and tried to help."

Too late, they were travelling at around 150 miles per hour as the under belly of the Liberator began slicing first through the heather, then into the moorland grass, peat and rock. The noise

This and opposite page: *Official USAAF pictures taken at the time. The wreckage was broken up and set on fire by the recovery team.*

was tremendous as metal panels were ripped away, followed by fuselage spars as the aircraft disintegrated.

"The thought struck me, that no one ever survives a crash like this and the next thing that I remembered was hearing voices — I was afraid to open my eyes, I thought that I was dead and I wasn't sure if I had gone up or down."

He was in an English hospital and he had no idea how he had got there, but it was a tremendous relief to him that he hadn't 'passed over'. A nurse told him that an ambulance was on its way to take him to a US Military Hospital. He had suffered some damage to his face and some bruising, but apart from shock, he had got away fairly light. Haopt had suffered more serious injuries to his face and had also a broken arm.

After leaving the hospital Jerry Najvar never saw 2nd Lieutenant Haopt again, nor did he ever hear of his whereabouts.

It is a puzzle as to why Haopt flew straight into the hillside when his engineer had warned him early enough. He was an experienced pilot with 176 hours flying time on Liberators, 90 hours of which had been flown by him in the last three months. Had the fraught take-off unnerved him? Flying conditions that day were appalling with overcast shrouding the high ground. In the official report visibility was given as being 3,900 yards, with haze, yet the cloud ceiling was 1,500 feet. It would seem that, although the fog had cleared some distance from the airfield, low cloud and haze had taken over in rendering flying conditions difficult.

Pressing schedules to deliver aircraft had, no doubt, pushed flying control at Burtonwood into going ahead. However, it was the crews who took all the risks.

Above: *A photograph of the throttle quadrant taken in recent times.*

*Blenheim IV, Z5870, 6 Anti-Aircraft Co-operation Unit, 12
Group, flying from Digby to Ringway, crashed below Crowden
Tower, Edale, July 3rd, 1941.*

Map reference 092871 • Map number 53

He was at a loose end after teatime on a pleasant July evening, so he decided to go for a walk on the moors. He wouldn't be required on duty again until 'Stand To' at dusk, and so John Hamer set off up onto the moors. His unit manned searchlights near Cowburn Tunnel and during the long light evenings it was pleasant to leave the wooden huts where they were billeted and stroll in the healthy air of the Pennines.

"I walked along a track which led from Barber Booth to Hayfield and on a whim struck off to my right over hte moors."

After about two miles John Hamer spotted a twin-engined aircraft on the ground. He hastened across to it and noted that it was a Blenheim, and that it was almost intact. There was along furrow scoured into the moorland where the bomber had ripped through the ground before coming to rest. In the shattered cockpit was the pilot, still strapped in his seat. The soldier went through the pilot's pockets looking for identification and saw from some papers that he was Polish. He made no further search of the wrecked fuselage assuming that the pilot was alone, and so he missed seeing the bodies of the other three airmen, the wireless operator and the two passengers. He trotted back down the moor to report his find and shortly he was returning with helpers.

The Blenheim, from an Anti-Aircraft Co-operation Unit based at Digby in Lincolnshire, was being flown to Ringway, Manchester for a major overhaul. For a group of young aircraftmen seeking a long weekend leave, it seemed

Above: *Polish pilot* **Nikky Plotek** (left) *and Flight Lieutenant Bunny Austin. This photograph was taken just three months before the accident which killed Nikky Plotek.*

like too good an opportunity for them to miss. By train, or hitching a ride by road, could be a long process, whereas a flight to a nearby aerodrome could take minutes. The pilot would need persauding, but he was a good chap, a Pole called Nikodem (Nikky) Plotek. Many of the pilots flying with the AACU were in fact Poles, as it was considered good practise for them in using the English language. Their flights in Lysanders and outdated Blenheims were controlled by the army. The purpose being to give gun-laying experience to the anti-aircraft defences.

Above: **Raymond Place**

Below: **William Franklin Kidd,** RCAF

One of the aircraftmen desiring a 'lift' home that Thursday afternoon was Ron Place, a flight mechanic who was a car salesman at a garage in Manchester (La Scala Motors) prior to the war. Another of the men hitching a lift on the blenheim that day was a Canadian, William Franklin Kidd. He had arrived in England just three months previously after training as a wireless operator — he was 21 years old. The youngest who was to loose his life that day was Wilfred Cottam, he was just 19 years old having joined the RAF at the age of 17. As a youngster he had always wanted to join the airforce and when war broke out he lied about his age and enlisted. He was Nikky Plotek's wireless operator.

Another airman attempted to hitch a lift on Blenheim Z5870 but failed. Three passengers were enough on a Blenheim but Nikky Plotek would have taken another. However, stores were unable to issue a further parachute and so aircraftman Broomhead could only look on as the aircraft took off — and curse his bad luck, he would have to 'thumb it' on the roads.

Conditions would have been cramped for the three passengers on board the Blenheim, but the journey would take less than an hour and so it was no real inconvenience. They were all dead in under 30 minutes.

Soldier John Hamer, who had been the

one to discover the tragedy, found himself assigned on guard duty at the

Above: *Wilfred Cottam*

wreck during the days prior to its recovery. "To amuse ourselves we found out how to cock and fire the twin machine guns in the turret on top of the fuselage. We discovered that the only way to stop them was to take a round out of the belt of ammunition."

One of the nights when John Hamer was amusing himself by hosing the night sky with threads of tracer bullets he succeeded in rousing the Home Guard in Hayfield and putting the whole district on alert. It didn't do much for his popularity with the local police, nor his commanding officer.

The wrecking of Blenheim Z5870 and deaths of all four men illustrates the strange quirks of fate: The aircraft had not been totally wrecked, there had been no fire and yet all had perished instantly. On the other hand, aircraft had crashed in seemingly similiar circumstances and the occupants had survived — even when the planes had completely disintegrated (see previous story). The pilot, Sergeant Plotek, had been caught in the old trap of meeting bad weather when flying west towards the Peninnes. He would have been flying at about 1,800 feet so as to keep sight of the ground, on that short hop. The wind vector would have pushed him slightly off track and the cloud shrouded mountains lay directly in his path.

He was a good pilot, gaining experience in the English language before transfering to one of the operational bomber squadrons. A former crew member of Plotek's, who had spent some 50 flying hours together with him, had found difficulty in understanding how a pilot as skilled as he could have died in such a way. But as may be seen from some of the accounts, both in this book and book two, some of the best pilots in the RAF ended up falling for the Pennine trap.

Hampden X3154, 106 Squadron RAF, on a cross-country exercise from Finningley, crashed December 21st, 1940.
Map reference 112835 ● Map key number 54

Just prior to the outbreak of the Second World War, 106 Squadron had been equipped with Hampdens. The Squadron operated in a training role during the first seven months of the war and that meant intensive training flights at night. Operating from Finningley, it also meant that numerous aircraft, manned by inexperienced crews, ended up on the Pennines. A few days before Christmas, 1940, Hampden X3154 took off on a cross-country training flight and crashed into the hills near Chapel-en-le-Frith. All the crew of four were killed and were as follows: Pilot Officer Michael Hubbard, Sergeants Perkins, Davy and Smith.

Above: *Michael Hubbard*

Vampire XE866, 4 Flying Training School, RAF, on a training flight from Worksop, crashed Stanage Edge, August 7th, 1957.
Map reference 230855 ● Map key number 55

The two-seater trainer (Vampire T Mk 11) took off from RAF Worksop at 8.35am and was due to return to base at 9.45am. On board were the instructor, Flying Officer P. R. Jones of Shrewsbury and pupil, Flying Officer D. Brett of Retford. They were three quarters of an hour overdue when Flying Officer Jones radioed Worksop to say that they were short of fuel. The Flying Controller at Worksop instructed them to descend to 6,000 feet and make a turn to Port, which would give them a straight course for base, passing over the city of Sheffield. The order was acknowledged and that was the final communication — they never arrived. The Mountain Rescue Service at Harpur Hill, Buxton, was alerted and also the police who

toured round in cars scouring the moors. At 6pm the following day wreckage was seen and police arrived at the scene of the accident. The aircraft was scattered over 200 yards of rocky ground on the boundary between the counties of Derbyshire and Yorkshire.

According to a policeman attending the site, the two men had been cut in half by the force of the impact and the upper parts were in Yorkshire, whilst the lower sections were in Derbyshire.

A Board of Inquiry was unsure of what had contributed to the accident and considered the possibility of the pilot making a descending turn instead of a level turn. The Station Commander was of the opinion that the pilot had misread the altimeter.

Wellington Z8980, 27 Operational Training Unit, RAF, on a night training flight from Lichfield, crashed Rudd Hill, July 17th, 1942.

Map reference 266828 • Map key number 56

With the successful television series 'Dad's Army' the role of the Home Guard in the last war has been held up as a source of good natured amusement. However, elements of those units were called upon to show initiative and bravery on occasions and they acquitted themselves well. When Wellington Z8980 hit the moorland and burst into flames, Sergeant J. F. Lowey of the Sheffield Home Guard set off with some of his men to render assistance. He was in command of a patrol of 20 men on Burbage Moor when the bomber crashed just after midnight. It was pouring with rain as Sergeant Lowey set off up the moor with half his contingent. Because of the heavy going over the peat bogs some of the older men dropped back — Lowey and two others reached the scene first. All the crew had scrambled clear, including the rear gunner who had a broken leg. They were all sprawled out around the blazing bomber and were in real danger of being consumed in the conflagration. Lowey and his two men pulled the five crew members clear and burned themselves severely in the process. Parachute harnesses were used to construct make-shift stretchers, and the injured flyers were carried off the moor to the waiting ambulances.

There had been an error in navigation and the city of Nottingham was wrongly identified as Leicester. Following the accident the crew parted company and three of them were killed later in the war in raids over Germany — they were: Pilot, Sergeant T. F. Thompson (FTR August 17th, 1944); Navigator, Pilot Officer J. W. Moore (FTR September 29th,1942); Wireless operator, Sergeant J. H. Levett; Air gunner, K. J. H. Harris (FTR January 4th, 1943); Air gunner, Sergeant J. H. Roden.

In January 1944, Sergeant Lowey received a Certificate of Gallantry for his part in the rescue of the injured airmen.

Blenheim Z5746, 2 Operational Training Unit, RAF, on a cross country exercise, crashed near Ox Stones, January 26th, 1941.

Map reference 278838 • Map key number 57

With the near desperate requirement for bomber crews, training schedules were often adhered to despite poor weather conditions. In a snow storm, January 1941, a trainee crew were wiped out in an accident when a 2 OTU Blenheim hit the high ground near Sheffield. The pilot was Sergeant John (Jack) Robson of Edinburgh; Navigator, Pilot Officer Ivor King Parry-Jones of Llanrwst; Wireless operator/ air gunner, Flight Sergeant Eric Brown of Dumfries.

Some of the inhabitants of Ringinglow heard the aircraft fly over and the bang as it hit the ground. That night a long trailer arrived at Ringinglow to collect the wreckage; earlier a team had gone up and retrieved the three bodies.

Left: **Jack Robson**   Right: **Eric Brown**

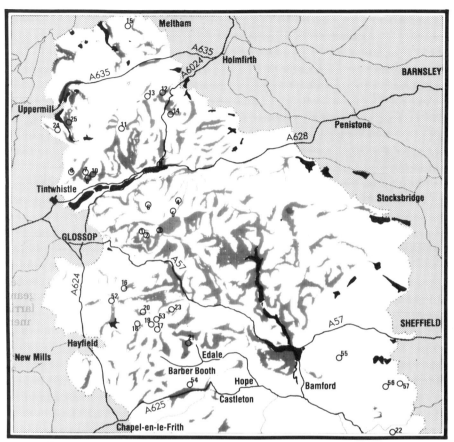

Crash sites covered in this book," *DARK PEAK AIRCRAFT WRECKS Book 1*":

1 LANCASTER KB993
2 C-47 SKYTRAIN
3 SUPERFORTRESS
4 BOTHA
5 DEFIANT N3378
6 BLENHEIM L1476
7 LANCASTER PA411
8 CHIPMUNK
9 HURRICANES
10 LIGHTNING P38
11 METEORS
12 SABRE RCAF
13 SWORDFISH
14 LIBERATOR 43-94841
15 FLYING FORTRESS
16 SABRES RAF

17 ANSON LN185
18 MILES HAWK
19 HARVARD
20 HAMPDEN AE381
21 HEYFORD
22 WELLINGTON Z8491
23 DRAGON RAPIDE
24 DAKOTA G-AHCY
25 MOSQUITO

52 LIBERATOR 42-52003
53 BLENHEIM Z5870
54 HAMPDEN X3154
55 VAMPIRE XE866
56 WELLINGTON Z8980
57 BLENHEIM Z5746

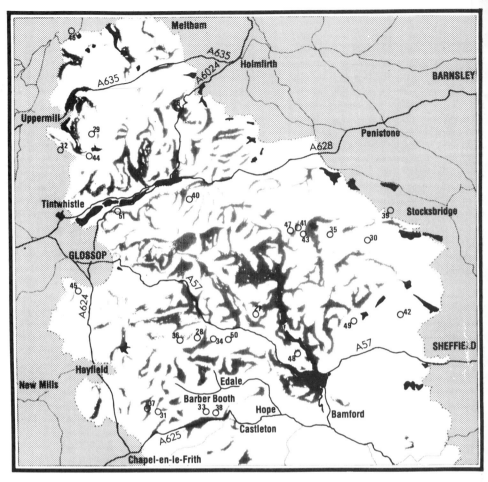

Crash sites covered in the second book "DARK PEAK AIRCRAFT WRECKS Book 2".

26 HAMPDEN L4055	39 ANSON N9912
27 DEFIANT N1766	40 WELLINGTON R1011
28 WELLINGTON W5719	41 OXFORD LX518
29 LYSANDER	42 WELLINGTON MF627
30 WELLINGTON DV810	43 V1 FLYING BOMB
31 THUNDERBOLT	44 TIGER MOTH
32 LIBERATOR PB4Y	45 MUSTANG P51D
33 SPITFIRE	46 BARRACUDA MD963
34 HALIFAX	47 CONSUL
35 STIRLING	48 METEOR RA487
36 ANSON N9853	49 VAMPIRE DH100
37 OXFORD HN594	50 WELLINGTON X3348
38 OXFORD NM683	51 BEAVER